ZANE
NELSON

SANITY STRATEGIES

FOR EVERYDAY MORMONS

Copyright © 1991 Zane Nelson
All rights reserved
Printed in the United States of America
Library of Congress Catalog Number: 91–073531
Sanity Strategies for Everyday Mormons
Covenant Communications, Inc.
Printed November 1991
ISBN 1–55503–363–6

Table of Contents

INTRODUCTION

When I reflect on our lives with their losses, confusions, and pains, I understand why we call this world a "vale of tears." The commandment to "endure to the end" can seem overwhelming. But life is not simply a bed of nails, and this book is not simply about pain management. Life can and should include those beautiful and rewarding moments implicit in the statement "Man is that he might have joy." A central message of this book is that moments of joy *are possible* in every life. But joy doesn't just happen; it occurs through a combination of effort and understanding.

This book is the result of many years of practice and teaching in individual and family therapy and of a life of work in the LDS Church. I have found my professional and religious experiences to be enormously rich sources of insight about the paths to happiness and fulfillment, and I want to share these insights. (Along with the knowledge and insight we can gain, however, we must also rely on faith to help us in those moments when life's pain threatens to overpower us.)

Many of the great truths of the gospel have been "rediscovered" by modern psychology. I have found in my practice that the principles of the gospel and the principles of good mental health (sanity strategies) are mutually reinforcing.

This book is an attempt to put these principles into layman's language and in so doing help you enlarge your understanding of how to keep your life in balance, improve your own mental health, help others in their struggles, and increase the ratio of joy to pain that you experience as you endure to the end

Sanity Strategy #1

Get it in Perspective

The principles we will talk about in this "Sanity Strategy" book could benefit anyone. However, I have observed a few peculiarities in our Mormon culture that make these principles especially important for us. Because of our tendency to focus on the ideal, it is vital to be cautious of unrealistic expectations and to get a grasp on the basic principles of good mental health in order to avoid such depressing pitfalls as perfectionism, pharasaism, and codependency.

If the glory of God is intelligence, then it is important for us to gain as much understanding as possible. As we gain more understanding, we actually become more godlike and are fulfilling our Heavenly Father's goal for us to grow and become more like him. However, just being aware of this goal can feel like pressure if we fail to keep it in perspective.

No one lives in the ideal right now in mortality, and we need to let go of the nagging feeling that somehow we should. Our challenge here is to learn to deal effectively with the realities of our imperfect world and imperfect selves so that we don't get bogged down, but can keep progressing toward the goal of becoming like our Father in Heaven.

Within our ranks, misunderstandings seem to be at the root of many common psychological problems. For example, many LDS people wrongly think that consistently accomplishing a great checklist of righteous activities constitutes righteousness. LDS women seem especially vulnerable to pressure regarding this never-ending list. The checklist attitude usually leads to an unhealthy emphasis on "doing" and less emphasis on "being."

There is also a tendency to want Church leaders to tell us exactly what should be on this checklist. A non-LDS patient of mine, a thoughtful, insightful, and sophisticated woman, once said to me, "You Mormons are so concerned about doing things absolutely right that you won't make decisions on your own. You have to have someone else [some authority figure] tell you what to do." After thinking about her comments and looking back on my service in leadership positions, I realized that what she said has much validity.

In New Testament times, Christ was critical of the Pharisees, in part, because of their rigidity and their adherence to the letter of the law at the expense of the Spirit. Many of us, instead of recognizing the need to live the spirit of the law, want a manual to tell us all the moves we should make; we want someone to tell us exactly how we should think, feel, and act. Yet we fail to realize the harm such a manual would do to individuality, imagination, and personal growth.

Indeed, we know that "it is not meet that man should be commanded in all things." To be commanded in all things would negate the growth that is possible through the exercise of free agency. Rigidly living according to a "letter of the law checklist" would also preempt our ability to live the higher laws of love.

When in a checklist mentality, many items on our "have to do" list may only be cultural traditions and personal preferences, yet we may view them to be as important as commandments. In fact we may actually believe that our acceptability to God hinges on our living up to many expectations that we have come to see as part of Church doctrine when in fact, they are nothing more than other people's ideas of how things should be done.

Any organization (and the Church is an organization) consists of three distinct components:

1. doctrines, creeds, and beliefs
2. traditions and practices
3. personal preferences and individual opinions

In the Church, it is helpful to keep these things separate. This is one of the reasons that Church leaders constantly recommend scripture study. If we are well grounded in the scriptural doctrines we can weed out of our lives the overwhelming array of ideas that other members may present as doctrines when they are only opinions or traditions. For instance, there is a huge difference between the law of chastity and the "law" some people propose of not kissing before marriage. We can rightfully be very exacting about keeping God's laws, but we also need to see the great difference between his laws and other people's opinions.

Many people concoct their own "gospel laws" in regard to practices that are only traditions, such as having white tablecloths to cover the sacrament. How we conduct our meetings and funerals, how we take care of the body after death, and even the day on which we honor the Sabbath (in Israel the Saints worship on Saturday) are all subject to differences in traditions in different countries. God has not set absolute laws about any of those things.

Traditions can add some continuity and consistency to our meetings, but it is important to recognize they are only practices. They are not connected to doctrines, nor are many of the personal opinions and preferences that we may often hear expounded as doctrine. The Church is made up of people, all of whom have their individual preferences, opinions, and weaknesses. The Church is a refuge from worldly values, but not from human foibles. Individual members sometimes build an entire belief system to justify their personal preferences, often while quoting scriptures or General Authorities out of context, about everything from prayer to pierced ears.

Because there are so many opinions and personal preferences, and because they may be so demanding and even contradictory in nature, trying to live up to them all does not lead to peace of mind. To turn our lives over to the opinions and preferences of other people is simply not God's will. If too many of these ideas become mandatory "should-do's" on our checklist of priorities, we will wind up stressed out, burned out, and enormously confused.

A girl whom I shall call Valerie came into my office recently. Like many LDS people, she has a strong committment to doing what is right and living the gospel. Unfortunately for Valerie, she really isn't well-grounded in Church doctrine. Therefore she relies heavily on what she is told by members of the Church. She was very distressed because a member had told her that since her father had been cremated instead of buried in the traditional Mormon way, it was very possible that his salvation was in jeopardy as well as the salvation of any family member who had helped make this "wrong decision." The body is a temple, the member had said, and cremation certainly doesn't respect that truth. To compound Valerie's problem, another member felt compelled to add that it was also disrespectful to pierce your ears. She said that if the Lord wanted us to wear pierced earrings we would be born with holes in our ears and that to decimate or mutilate the body in any way would certainly be against God's will. Because Valerie believed these women, she had been suffering unnecessary guilt and anxiety. She was more than relieved when I assured her that these members' opinions on those issues were not Church doctrine.

The importance of being well-grounded in the doctrines of the Church is clearly essential to keep from being easily influenced and even depressed by the opinions of well-meaning members. It is an important "Sanity Strategy" to sort out the items on our checklists and analyze our beliefs and assumptions. Non-doctrinal beliefs can be the source of much of our stress, and we can weed this source of stress out, because they are based only on opinions or preferences.

This book offers many strategies to help solve such problems that are inherent in our culture and inherent in the human condition. If you have ever felt overwhelmed with the many demands that seem to be part of the LDS lifestyle, this book will help you. We will discuss the importance of biological health and good feelings, examine the role of behaviors and thoughts, and learn proven methods for resolving negative thoughts. In a helpful, straightforward manner we will look at ten tested strategies for achieving mental health and joy. These strategies will help us to better understand the importance of free agency and balance in the joy equation.

Sanity Strategy #2

Don't Try to Tighten a Bolt with an Eggbeater

In his book, *Stress Reduction for Mormons*, John C. Turpin tells of an exhausted woman who came to his office in a state of total burnout. She had lived according to the false belief that she should give her all to the Church and her family and that it would be selfish to take time to meet her own needs. She was physically depleted to the point of possible chemical depression. She had drawn away from the Lord and resented the Church. A new counseling technique alone would not have made her feel better. She needed to solve her physical problems first. By beginning there, over a period of months she was able to regain her physical strength, *then* learn new coping skills. Her good feelings about herself and the Church eventually returned stronger than ever.

Solve Biological Problems First

Physiological problems are often a root cause of many common emotional disorders, depression included. Any attempt to change the way a human thinks or acts must include an understanding of potential physiological factors. For example, a track coach, no matter how encouraging he is and how much expertise he has, will never be able to teach a severely anemic person to run well unless the anemia is treated first. To work on running techniques without solving a physical problem would be like trying to tighten a bolt with an eggbeater. Similarly, no matter how competent the counselor, a patient will never do well if some physical problem exists that affects his thoughts, moods, attitudes, energy or general reasoning.

The Physiological Basis of Mental Health

Our bodies are very intricate, integrated systems. A number of complex hormonal and chemical mechanisms may need to be evaluated and possibly regulated in order to have proper mental functioning. Of course, not every mental illness has a physiological basis, but physiological components that could contribute to mental problems need to be evaluated when a person is experiencing emotional or mental problems.

A number of mental disorders are caused primarily by physiological problems. Often these physiological problems involve chemicals called neurotransmitters. Through laboratory studies, many different chemicals, along with stimulating and regulatory hormones, can be evaluated to learn if the body is lacking any of them.

Counseling is a needless uphill battle when one is fighting a physiological problem that could be easily corrected by medication. It is not uncommon in our culture to hear of people who resist needed help and refuse to take medication. They may conclude that abuse and overuse of medications in our society means all medication is bad, or they may have the false belief that if they trusted in the Lord enough they would never need medication. Yet evidence shows that because of wise use of medication, many people have had their lives turned around. Many have felt led by the Spirit to particular doctors that have been able to diagnose and prescribe accurately.

Some time ago, a lady in her mid-fifties came in to see me after much prodding by her family. She had literally been sitting around for years doing nothing. She had little or no energy, no hope, no ambition, no zest for life. She was simply waiting to die. At my insistence, a series of routine blood tests was completed. She was found to be extremely hypothyroid (which means she had an underactive thyroid). A thyroid supplement totally reversed her world. She started cleaning her house, joining clubs, and participating in Church activities. All the counseling in the world could not have accomplished this miracle because it could not have corrected the root problem.

It isn't unnatural for a person to hesitate taking medication for fear of negative side effects, but most medications used to correct physiological problems do not create physical addictions or psychological dependencies. Instead, these medications replenish a deficient chemical in the body, as insulin does for a diabetic. They can often help a person get through a depressive period rapidly solving the problem completely. On the other hand, when a chemical imbalance is present, changes brought about by counseling can take a long time, if they ever occur at all. Whether chemically imbalanced or not, a patient does not learn a new way of thinking or acting overnight. If a physical problem exists, the whole improvement process can be greatly accelerated through medication.

When dealing with a mental or emotional problem, we need to ask what kind of damage is being done to our spiritual health, careers, and relationships; then we must ask ourselves if we can afford to let these suffer for longer than is necessary. We also need to remember that our most important relationship is the one with ourselves. A speedy resolution of an emotional problem helps us maintain a good self-image, which in turn diffuses serious complications that might have come along due to self-degradation.

Physicians and psychologists have made great strides in explaining relevant physiological mechanisms to the general public. In so doing, they have lessened the stigma associated with physiological imbalances and, indeed, with psychological problems in general. We are nearly to the point where there will be no greater stigma attached to the chemical imbalances that cause psychological and emotional problems than to those that cause thyroid problems or diabetes.

Not only has more been done to educate people in the last several years, but mental health professionals are becoming more skilled in the actual intervention and treatment required to treat complex psychological and physiological imbalances. For example, in the mid-1970s, the electroencephalograph became computerized. Now professionals can carefully evaluate brain dysfunctions, temperament problems resulting from brain injuries, as well as genetic, developmental, and other subtle problems causing personality and mental disorders.

Cumulatively, these changes have resulted in help for many people who before might have allowed their lives to be disrupted or destroyed rather than seek treatment because of the negative stigma attached to mental illness. It is heartening to note that more and more people are accepting the fact that proper medical intervention may be critical for those experiencing biochemical difficulties and that many psychological problems are physically based.

Sanity Strategy #3

Masking, Unmasking: Fine-Tune Your Feelings

The second fundamental cause of emotional and mental problems is feelings; therefore, learning to understand and deal effectively with feelings is an essential part of good mental health.

In counseling, when I stress the importance of working toward good feelings, I am referring to what I call "core feelings," feelings that are private and deep. These feelings involve emotions not usually tapped in typical daily communications such as talk about the weather or greetings on the street.

If good feelings and proper physiological functioning are present, positive issues and symptoms are usually evident. Conversely, if negative feelings are present or some physiological breakdown is impairing emotional health, negative issues and symptoms are presented. For example, if a couple shares feelings of love, self-esteem, and charity, they are not likely to be arguing about issues such as balancing the checkbook, doing the dishes, or getting dinner ready on time (although there will be discussions). Thus they have no need for a counselor. When problems occur, a study of our deep feelings is essential to finding a resolution.

However, when negative feelings are present, negative issues and behaviors surface and become troublesome Negative feelings are often manifested in physical symptoms. Our particular physiological weaknesses and propensities most likely determine which physical symptoms we will suffer. For example, in some people, depression and stress tend to show up as colitis; in others, they appear as headaches or stomachaches. On the following page is a list of both positive and negative feelings with their respective issues.

Positive Feelings	**Positive Issues**
Love	Agreement of Discipline
Acceptance	Balanced Budget
Openness	Good Sex Life
Honesty	Recreational Togetherness
Comfortableness	Creative Conversation
Security	Good Health
Togetherness	
Negative Feelings	**Negative Issues**
Anger	Money Differences
Indifference	Poor Sex Life
Feeling Judged	Substance Abuse
Gauardeness	Suicide Threats
Avoidance	Physical Violence
Fear	Yelling
Criticalness	Name Calling
Loneliness	Physical/Somatic Problems

Dealing with Feelings Before Facts

Our feelings are directly connected with our thoughts and actions. In order to change negative feelings to positive feelings, we have to change our thoughts and actions. Nevertheless, we need to first direct our attention to feelings and leave thoughts and actions until later. There are good reasons for this. When people come to me wanting help to overcome problems in their lives, they often state their problems in terms of the symptoms they are experiencing. Usually they think that to overcome their problems they need to rid themselves of the symptoms. I have learned, however, that if we only deal with the symptoms and fail to understand the *feelings* from which the symptoms stem (the root problem), the symptoms will never be resolved.

For example, a wife may say to her husband, who is in the bishopric, "You never spend time with me." If the conversation then focuses on the amount of time he is away rather than her feelings about his absence, they will make little progress toward a resolution. Whether he was gone every night last week or only one night is less central than her specific fears, apprehensions, and insecurities. It is her *feelings* about the issues that need to be addressed. The most productive therapy usually occurs when people are able to talk openly about their feelings while holding the facts and specific issues in the background.

When people first come into my office, their inclination is to mask their deepest feelings while pushing forward a number of issues, many of which may be irrelevant. Most often, they mistakenly believe that a discussion of troubling issues will provoke an examination of the "principles" that are supposedly holding them back. They often play the principles game—"Don't you think people should?" They do not realize that principles are always right to the person who holds them and that to argue principles is often a simple avoidance of real feelings.

The temptation to fall into this trap is doubled for conscientious Church members because we are so committed to principles. We seem to espouse not only the principles of all "upstanding principled people," but hundreds of other principles as well. Statements meant to reform one's spouse like "We really should read the scriptures and pray regularly together" or "You know we should work on our food storage, and your attitude is the reason we don't" are destructive rather than constructive to a relationship, just as are general statements such as "You have to agree we should spend more quality time together" or "It's obvious we should be more frugal with our money."

A husband and wife came to see me for marriage counseling. They often argued about principles and issues. One of his main complaints was her housekeeping. During one session he told me, in front of his wife, how he had watched a pizza box lay on the kitchen table for five days. He would walk by the pizza box every day keeping score. He used this as a primary example of her inadequacy in housekeeping. Then he would shore up his arguments with principles such as "Cleanliness is next to godliness" and "The Spirit of the Lord cannot be in an unkempt house." The issues in this example are small, but they created a major problem for this couple.

Let's look closer at the above example. How much time would it have required of him on his way out to simply drop the pizza box into the garbage can that sat next to his car? Instead, he was trying to justify his bad feelings with evidence. If this husband had feelings of love for his wife, he would be trying to find ways to help her and support her in overcoming the bad housekeeping rather than looking for reasons to justify his bad feelings.

Another problem with discussing principles rather than feelings is that principles often conflict in some way. A man who has just declared bankruptcy may say, "Don't you feel we should be forgiving of debt and help others in real need?" The other party may respond, "Don't you feel people should meet up to their obligations and responsibilities in life?" All such "principle" arguments may be true, but because they ignore deep feelings, they complicate the problem instead of resolving it. The "principle" may also be in the category of personal opinion, tradition, or preference, and should all the more be covered by the principle of free agency. No progress can be made in the discussion until the feelings behind the statements of principle are explored and understood.

After the feelings are recognized, the next step is to learn to deal with them. In order to deal with feelings, we must first be able to interpret them. We need to realize that many of the things we *feel* are not necessarily facts. The most common disorder I see is depression. This is usually accompanied by problems with self-esteem where the sufferer has feelings of worthlessness and a poor self-concept. In reference to themselves, sufferers will use adjectives such as ugly, stupid, fat, worthless, unlovable, and unpopular. Sometimes it is immediately obvious that the sufferer's feelings have little to do with reality. An attractive person *can* have feelings of ugliness; to them, their "ugliness" is very much a reality.

Reality testing and value clarification are ways a counselor can help patients sort out fact from fiction in regard to their feelings. Reality testing will be discussed on page 43, and a discussion and explanation of Value Clarification can be found on page 46.

To Mask or Not to Mask? That Is the Question

One tool we all use for managing feelings is called masking. We've often heard the expression "Put on a happy face." In some quarters, this is written off as phoniness and superficiality, but I believe masking our true feelings is appropriate when we are in public. Indeed, the benefits of masking become obvious when you think of sitting at work sobbing your eyes out because of a serious problem with your family.

People don't like to be around those that always seem unhappy. Many people who come in to see me have consistently failed to mask their negative feelings and have consequently found themselves isolated from others. In fact, depressed people, who are some of the most isolated, are often the least able to put on a mask.

Virtually everyone occasionally puts on an emotional mask. It is functional and appropriate to minimize emotional problems when we are in public. Don't misunderstand. In saying that there is a time to mask or minimize impulses and inclinations, I'm not advocating the systematic deception of others. I am recommending a type of compartmentalization. When at work or out in public, don't flood the compartmental system. There are times for letting feelings out just as there are "teaching moments." We need to learn to recognize those times.

If we are feeling deeply disturbed, when and with whom do we dare take our masks off? The answer varies with the severity of the problem, the strength of friendships, and the chances of getting good advice. Sometimes, with the right people and in appropriate places, it is all right to "take off our emotional masks" even though it may feel awkward and uncomfortable. Emotional intimacy is impossible if we always keep our masks on and in counseling it is *critical* that unmasking take place for proper evaluation and therapy. It should, however, be done with discrimination and discernment.

Finding a balance between masking and unmasking is not always easy. Many of our relationships are surface relationships. Unmasking, or trying to get others to unmask is not appropriate in these relationships. However, to establish close relationships, unmasking, or sharing of deep feelings, is appropriate and necessary. To be sensitive in important and necessary relationships, we should look beyond the surface and learn when and how to communicate our deepest feelings.

Appropriately sharing feelings is important to good mental health. A great many people have learned to be passive, and as a result, they tend to ignore their feelings. They wear their public mask when they should take it off. "Gunnysacking" feelings—storing them up for long periods of time—results in an eventual explosion and can also result in physical problems, such as ulcers, high blood pressure, or headaches.

Sensitivities: Trace Them Back to Feelings

Sensitivities are also a derivative of feelings, and they too vary greatly from person to person. In many ways, sensitivities are the bridge between the way people feel about others and the way they feel about themselves. Some people are extremely sensitive to things like height, weight, religion, race, and certain words. Most of us are considerate enough to respect other people's sensitivities even if it means going out of our way. It is true that some people are overly sensitive and very easily offended (too easily maybe), but if we are to be Christlike, we have an obligation not to hurt these people when we find out where their sensitivities lie.

When the Corinthian Christians asked Paul whether they should adopt the practice of eating the meat that had been offered to idols, Paul said the practice in itself would neither hurt them nor help them. But then he said, "Take heed lest by any means this liberty of yours become a stumblingblock to them that are weak. . . . Wherefore, if meat make my brother to offend, I will eat no flesh while the world standeth."(1 Cor. 8:9, 13.) This not only warns us not to prey on the sensitivities of others, but it also reminds us that while we are free to choose how we act, we are responsible for the consequences of those actions. If we act responsibly, we will be alert to words, mannerisms, or behaviors that offend or distract certain people. In this way, we can honor people's sensitivities and they, in turn, will learn to honor ours. Consideration toward others takes relatively little energy, and yet it goes far toward circumventing communication breakdowns.

Sometimes our own sensitivities are not clear to us. One of my patients who had a difficult struggle with her weight was finally brought to the realization of her oversensitivity by a cute, but provocative, incident with one of her children. For obvious reasons the word "fat" had become a dirty word in her house. While the family was having dinner at a friend's house, her child brought his plate to her and asked, "Mom, would you cut some of the chubby off my steak?"

Some people are overly sensitive toward the idea of therapy. They see the suggestion of a need for therapy as an insult. Those who come to a therapist without understanding that therapy is an opportunity to grow and gain more insights put themselves in a double-bind. If the therapist tells them they need to come in once a week for six months, they think they are being told that they are very sick and will be for a long time. On the other hand, if the therapist tells them to come back every other month because they are doing fine, they think the therapist doesn't like them and doesn't want to see them very often. Because of their super-sensitivities, many people never win in the therapy game.

Feelings are indeed the hinge on which joy and misery swing. Although problems that cause us misery are manifested in unpleasant symptoms, the symptoms are actually a manifestation of bad feelings. We must first address and understand these bad feelings, not just the symptoms, if we are to find relief from the symptoms and have peace and joy.

Sanity Strategy #4

Explore Your Gunny Sacks and Wooden Legs

The "As If" Principle: We Live It, We Understand It

William James, a 19th century philosopher, talked about the "as if" principle. James said that if you want to feel and think something, act "as if" you *do* feel and think that way. If you want to be brave, act as a brave person would act. Eventually you will begin to feel brave. To put it in a Christian perspective, if you want to be a loving person, act loving. You may not think and feel loving in the beginning, but if you continue the loving behavior, you will soon begin to feel loving, as well as loved.

It is true that feelings are very difficult to change, even when they are acknowledged and discussed. But feelings are often responsive to behaviors. What we need to do is convert bad feelings into positive feelings. Good behaviors usually lead to good feelings, whereas bad behaviors promote bad feelings.

I knew an LDS woman who, for personal reasons, felt very angry at her bishop. She told me this anger caused many problems, one of which involved her desire to get a temple recommend. She knew that during the interview she would be asked if she supported and sustained the general and local authorities of the Church. I asked her if she did support and sustain her bishop. She said she did everything she was ever asked to do and did not talk behind his back, but she simply did not like him. I told her that sustaining and supporting a person does not necessarily require liking him. Liking her bishop would certainly make her relationship with him more pleasant, but liking him is not mandatory to sustaining him.

She went to her interview, and when the question of sustaining the general and local authorities came up, she said, "Yes, I do sustain the authorities."

The bishop, who knew of this woman's negative feelings for him asked, "Do you sustain me?"

She replied "Yes, I sustain you; I just don't like you." Her honest and sincere reply opened the door for communication. Eventually she and the bishop resolved many of their differences. She was able to reconcile with the bishop because she had not acted on her negative feelings by criticizing him behind his back or by ignoring his requests.

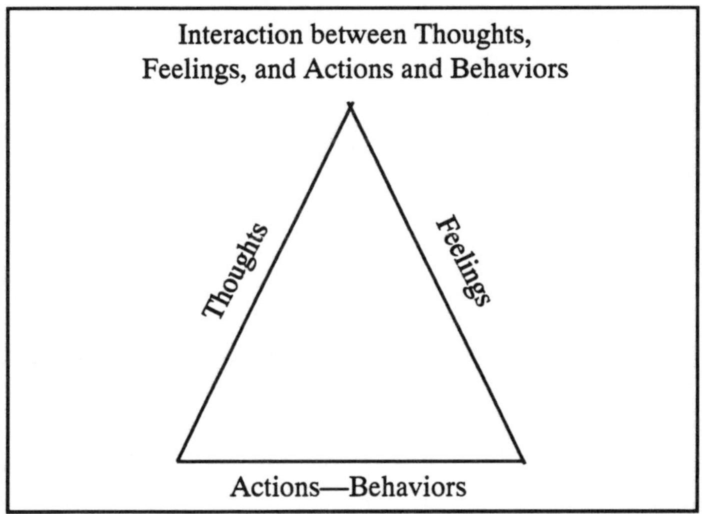

In mental health, one of the things a therapist encourages a person suffering from depression to do is to act "un-depressed." (This is assuming the individual has been checked for a chemical imbalance, that would have to be corrected before therapy could be effective.)

Many people respond to feelings of depression by talking of nothing else but their low spirits. It does not take long before they notice that people who once enjoyed their company begin avoiding them. Understanding why this happens is not difficult; human beings naturally try to avoid depressing situations, especially when they see no sign that the situation will improve. One key that will help relieve this problem is for the person suffering from depression to act as if he is not depressed.

Those suffering from depression often lay in bed long after they wake up. If and when they do get up, they mope around the house thinking of nothing other than how bad they feel. This, of course, isolates them socially, which only makes them feel worse. Emotionally healthy people, on the other hand, get up soon after they wake up. They get showered and dressed and then go out and get involved with the people at work, at the health club, or in in a civic activity. They are involved in welfare projects, home or visiting teaching, or in being thoughtful and considerate neighbors. They do not always feel like doing these things at the start, but they do them because they know being active will make them feel better.

It is a given that people suffering from depression will not feel like doing any of these things. However, if they can force themselves to get involved, even if it is in just one activity that gets them out of the house, chances are—if they keep at it long enough—they will begin to beat their depression and feel better.

Of course, this does not apply to chemical depressions. People who are chemically depressed can wear themselves out doing all the right things from morning till night and still feel depressed. But for those chemically in balance, positive behavior really can change feelings for the better.

President Kimball made famous the saying: "Do it." It does not matter if we don't *feel* like behaving like an emotionally healthy person—to begin with we just have to "do it"!

Effort Is Essential to Change and Growth

The key to beating depression through a change in behavior is effort. If you are going to be successful at becoming an active, happy person, you have to marshall your efforts to change your behavior. *That is, be willing to practice discipline, delay gratification, suffer, and push past the natural man.*

While we are capable of making major changes, we often don't, because we tend to be lazy and fear the unknown. We often want our world to change, but not ourselves! If I didn't believe that people *could* change their actions, thoughts, and perceptions of reality, I could not tolerate my field of work. As a therapist, I admire people who have the courage to confront themselves in an open and assertive way and are willing to work for the necessary changes within themselves that are necessary to their happiness.

Change rarely happens all at once, but when it occurs, it is often accompanied by pain and discomfort. Positive change will never be experienced by people who have no tolerance for discomfort and are too emotionally fragile to honestly confront their weaknesses and problems.

Take the example of a skier. A good skier has fallen countless times. It is the bad skiers who have only fallen a few times. The good skier learns from his falls. The bad skier has not dared to fall enough to learn anything. This skier will usually quit the sport, explaining that skiing is too difficult and too dangerous. The good skier learns from his falls and eventually gets so good that he falls very little—but not until he has fallen countless times. The bad skier, who had no less ability to ski than the good skier, became a victim to his falls and gave up.

Most "victims of life" have failed to recognize that they have been granted free agency. They do not understand that they have the right to choose. It is choosing that takes us out of the victim role and makes us responsible for our own lives. People in victim roles usually ignore their own responsibility in the situation; they feel they have no control over their environment. If these people are honest with themselves, they will realize that actually they can have as much control over their environment as anyone else. The problem may be their impatience and unwillingness to work and suffer enough to gain that control.

In his book *Faith Precedes the Miracle*, President Kimball presents faith as an action word. Faith denotes effort toward something true in which you have hope but cannot yet see. When we first muster the faith to try something new or to make a change, we may not be able to do the thing we are trying to do well at all. But it is of paramount importance that we keep trying to do it anyway.

As we put forth the effort necessary to live the principles conducive to good mental health, living the principles will eventually become a habit. Many have borne witness that they gained their testimony of the law of tithing only after they lived the law of tithing. Confucius once said, "I see something, I know it. I hear something, I learn it. I live something, I understand it." Whether we feel like it or not, we must *live* the principles of good mental health or we will not *have* good mental health. The good news is that the more we live them, the more we will feel like it, because the rewards are so great.

The "Wooden Leg" Alternative to Changing Behavior

A common problem I see among those suffering from depression is the tendency to develop excuses rather than go through the discomfort required to change behavior. This is a similar problem in physical health care. Suppose that after an operation on your knees, you use a wheelchair until the doctor says, "It's time to walk with a walker and start some exercises." You respond, "It will hurt. I won't try to walk until it won't hurt anymore." Would you ever walk again? Never.

I call a medical condition that one uses as an excuse and that *unnecessarily* impairs mental health a "wooden leg." Quite simply, some people with behavioral, but not medical, problems claim they have medical problems in order to avoid the pain and effort of changing their behavior. A good example of this is a person who is obese from overeating, but claims to have a metabolic imbalance.

When a man has a wooden leg, he has an excuse. When asked to dance, he says, "Gee, I'd love to, but you see I have this wooden leg. You don't expect me to participate with this severe handicap, do you?" The man's wife also benefits from his wooden leg, if she chooses. Her story is "I'd also love to dance, but my husband's wooden leg makes that impossible."

One acquaintance of mine has a wife who is manic-depressive. This man says he would like to get a better job but laments that if he switched to a new company with new insurance benefits, his wife's condition would be deemed pre-existing. He says this is why he remains at his old job.

In saying that wooden legs are used as excuses, I am certainly not implying that people with these excuses do not have any real pain. They do. But as with many illnesses in the body, the pain does not immediately reveal its source. We can compare this pattern: If a child comes in with chicken pox, the red spots are not so much the disease as they are *symptoms* of the disease. The real problem is the exposure to a virus and the immune system's inability to resist that virus.

The challenge with wooden legs—excuses—is to discover the real source of the pain that has become an obstacle to changing the patient's behavior. A lady we will call Sue came to me stating that her major goal was to lose weight. Sue was a single mother in her mid-thirties and had several children at home. She had had a weight problem even before her divorce, but since the divorce she had reached 350 pounds. While she had stated that one of the main reasons for coming to see me was to lose weight, we soon realized that her weight had become her wooden leg. She eventually admitted that because of her religious background, the most terrifying thing she could imagine was to be sexually involved outside of marriage. This was more terrifying to her than death. In time, she realized that her weight was her insulation from men and from sexual contact. She reasoned, "Who would be attracted to a 350-pound woman?"

We worked on her self-confidence. Eventually she realized that women could be thin and virtuous as well. With this knowledge she was able to give up her wooden leg. Consequently, she began losing weight, started socializing, and became a much more outgoing and happy person.

Clearly, some people cling fiercely to their handicaps as a means of avoiding other problems. One of my patients initially came to me in such a lethargic state that he could barely function in his day-to-day life. Routine laboratory work led us to a diagnosis of hypothyroidism. An internist prescribed some thyroid medication, and within a few weeks the man was active and more energetic. When he became capable of going back to work, he suddenly chose to quit the medication. Within a few weeks he was back in his chair, totally unresponsive to the world. He claimed that if God had made him hypothyroid, that was simply a cross he must bear. If God wanted him cured, he would change his metabolism. In my opinion, this man was not demonstrating faith but was using the pretense of faith to justify his desire to remain inactive and not work.

Wooden legs grow from fear and from lack of committment to life, but also from ignorance. For example, since most people understand something about diabetes, few have problems accepting insulin as a legitimate means of controlling the disorder. However, when people find out they are out of balance in such things as serotonin, dopamine, norepinephrine, thyroid, or any of the regulatory or stimulating hormones, they often resist corrective action because they do not understand what these things are or what they do. Since many people avoid that which frightens them, they often reject that which could help them live happier lives.

The Programs which Run Our Feelings and Behaviors

Thoughts are programs that run our feelings and behaviors much like computer software programs run the hardware on a computer. However, since thoughts are elusive and hard to pin down, therapists find it much easier to focus on changing behaviors. As discussed above, changing behaviors can change thoughts. This does not mean therapists will ignore the thought processes behind the behaviors. In fact, reality testing, value clarification, models of respect, and transactional analysis are all methods a therapist may use to help people analyze and evaluate their thought patterns. In the following pages we will first discuss behaviorial changes and then move on to thought processes.

Concentrate on Behaviors

I see many people whose obsessions with one thing or another are running their lives. An obsession is, by definition, often a repugnant or unreasonable thought or idea that becomes repetitive and may lead to compulsive behaviors. I have said before that thoughts and feelings aren't easy to change, but it is necessary to overcome obsessions to attain a state of mental health.

One exercise I sometimes like to use is rather absurd but strongly demonstrates that changing behavior is often more effective than trying to change thoughts. I have people close their eyes and see an elephant in their mind's eye. I have them describe the elephant in as much detail as they possibly can. After the thought is imprinted on the brain, I tell them not to have any more thoughts or ideas about elephants. Usually, they will try to think of other things and do the best they can, but within moments they fail. Once an idea is strongly implanted in the mind it is difficult to shake it. How do I help people get rid of an obsession? Do I just tell them not to think of elephants anymore? That's obviously a futile step. No, in fact, I probably will not even mention thoughts; I will focus instead on behaviors. If their obsession *were* elephants, I would ask them, Do you have to go to circuses and zoos? No, they can go other places. Do they have to read books about elephants? No, they can read books about other things. Do they have to watch "Tarzan" reruns? No, they can go to movies about a million other things besides elephants. What about words that come out of their mouths? Can they avoid talking about elephants? Of course they can. The point is that we treat obsessions by focusing on behavior. If a person eliminates all behaviors related to their obsession, the obsession becomes less a part of their thoughts and they begin to function more normally.

A Plan for Confronting Obsessions and False Belief Systems

As mentioned earlier, it is beneficial for any of us to look at our beliefs, or old "programs," and analyze those that cause us conflicts. These beliefs were formed when we were children without enough life experience or background to analyze, judge, or evaluate the teachings received from parents, teachers, or other adults. Many of these teachings are based on the categories of traditions, opinions, and personal preferences we discussed in Chapter 1, but they may have been taught to us as "gospel." It is helpful to remember as we analyze our beliefs that the word "*choose*" has power. As adults we have the power of choice—we can *choose* to change those beliefs or thoughts that we discover to be false, that are no longer helpful, or that are self-defeating. Parents do not set out to give their children neurotic or self-defeating ideas, but even so they may pass on beliefs that they received from their parents, which are actually myths. Some of our beliefs did not come from direct teachings, but may be a result of faulty conclusions or assumptions that we made as children. For example, when Reed, a man in his early forties, first came to see me, he was rather evasive about sharing his feelings. He was a large, jovial man who seemed to fit well the stereotypical "jolly fat man" role.

He finally admitted that he never let anyone see the sad, hurt, fearful, or rejected side of him. Because of beliefs he had developed over the years, like "Never let anybody see your vulnerable side or they will hurt you," "Avoid close, intimate feelings because they make you vulnerable," and "If you make people laugh, they will like you," he found it nearly impossible to develop deep relationships with anybody.

These beliefs kept Reed from having a full and happy life and interfered with his marriage relationship. Even in his relationship with his children, Reed was never serious and never showed his soft, tender side. At work, people became annoyed with his rather flippant, cavalier style.

Basically, Reed's personality was unbalanced because of his false belief system. While his humorous, joking manner was rather attractive at first, it eventually began to wear on people. After talking it out, Reed was able to realize he needed to find a better balance between too much humor and no humor at all. He was also able to recognize that some of the beliefs and conclusions he had made were erroneous and problematic.

How do we change beliefs? We can ask ourselves two questions any time we are experiencing conflicts in ourselves: What assumption am I making about this situation or person? and Am I certain this assumption is based on fact? When we identify the assumption or belief on which we are basing our actions, we will be able to detect the faulty element of that assumption or belief and make corrections. We believe something because we think it is true. To quit believing it, we must see clearly that it is not true and sense emotionally the damage the false belief is doing to us. Change is better effected when both logic and feelings are involved.

However, it is possible for us to elevate ourselves past negative *behaviors,* and remain stuck in negative or neurotic *thinking patterns.* Consequently, we will still experience unhappiness. We may be action oriented and engaged in many beneficial activities. Yet, much like those who wallow in unearned guilt, we can still focus our thoughts on our shortcomings and on an endless list of sins of omission.

If we fall into this trap we may harbor deep feelings of resentment because of our own inability to do everything right. We can be angry, critical, and judgmental of others whom we see as flippant, irresponsible, unspiritual, or otherwise lacking. We can project our self-defeating "critical parent ego" onto others and see them as the source of our problems. This leads to viewing others in a critical, double binding way.

To confront false belief systems that cause negative or neurotic thinking, write a list of beliefs, conclusions, assumptions, and values you presently hold. Break these beliefs down into categories like general philosophy of life, marriage, God, church, work, money, sex, men, women, children, and self-concept.

For example, as a youth, I drew a faulty conclusion about the correlation between size and intelligence. I thought big people were dumb people. I noticed that in movies and other media, large people were often depicted as mentally slow. Now I stand about six feet five. It took me until my early adulthood to realize that this was a stereotype and that there was no relationship between size and intelligence whatsoever. By doing this exercise we may be able to discover many such faulty conclusions we have drawn in our lives.

Beliefs can be effectively and logically evaluated through a psychological point of view I like to call the integrated adult (see Chapter 7). This evaluation may take the assistance of someone who can aid us in being objective because our beliefs may be so rooted as part of our basic philosophy that they seem almost holy. We may accept them without consideration and may not recognize the problems they are causing us. The old adage "Anything worth doing is worth doing well" is a great example. It sounds inoccuous. However, if really applied to life, this belief can be self-limiting and debilitating and would preclude doing anything just for the fun of it. What if you cleaned your house, gave a speech, skied, or prepared a meal only when you could do it well? We have to accept the fact that we are sometimes limited by time, experience, and physical inabilities, and that some things are simply not important enough to merit the time and attention it would take to do them well.

As you can see, some of our beliefs sound logical, but may be causing turmoil in our lives. Some of our faulty belief systems may be about ourselves, such as the one I had about large people, or they may be aimed at other people. For example, a sexually abused woman may believe all men are bad. This faulty belief will interfere with any possibilities of a positive, fulfilling relationship with a man.

To become aware of and understand the effects these beliefs have on our lives may be difficult without the help of an outside person who can see with an objective eye. However, I strongly believe that because God granted us free agency and the power to choose, we aren't allowed the excuse of "being a victim." We do not have to be emotionally attached to, bigoted by, or prejudiced by our past beliefs. Through confronting and carefully examining our beliefs, we can choose new, more effective, more realistic ways of thinking and believing.

The following examples give a taste of the kinds of response I see when people examine their beliefs:

Old Beliefs	New Beliefs
Work:	Work:
Anything worth doing is worth doing well.	Some things are worth doing well. Other things we do just because they need to be done . . . and then there are things we do just for the fun of it.
Self-concept:	Self-concept:
I'm just like Dad.	I have Dad's eyes and sense of humor, but I am different in other respects such as. . . .
God:	God:
God loves me only if I'm good.	God loves me always and wants me to be happy. I'm happier when I'm good.

Life: Good things never last.	Life: Things change, but even so I can enjoy the moment.
Sex: Sex is for procreation.	Sex: Sex is for many things: communication, bonding, expression of love, and procreation.

Take the time today to do this exercise yourself. Write down all the beliefs you can pinpoint, and spend the time necessary to analyze and decide from your present point of view which ones need to be re-worded and changed. You will be amazed at the sense of freedom you will feel!

Sanity Strategy #5

You Fought for Free Agency—Now Enjoy It!

Free agency is an integral and critical principle that we must honor. Although it is often not easy to accept this principle, we become devilish if we do not honor it. To try to control anyone but ourselves is not God's will, but Satan's.

We fought a great war in heaven over the freedom of choice. We must remember this when we have the urge to coerce someone into acting or thinking a particular way. We have the responsibility to encourage, admonish, and teach correct principles, but in the end, it is each individual's personal right and obligation, to choose.

When we fought the great war in heaven, a third of the hosts of heaven sided with Lucifer in wanting to deny man free agency. Siding against God and wanting to deny man his free agency seems like an illogical thing to do, but from my experience as a therapist, I have come to understand why so many spirits did so. I believe they chose Satan's plan because they feared the responsibility free agency would bring. They feared the freedom to make wrong choices and the consequences that would follow.

Helping Versus Controlling

As I watch parents deal with children, spouses with spouses, and friends with friends, I recognize an innate desire (perhaps part of the natural man?) to control other people's lives.

Yet if we take control of other people's lives, we also become responsible for them. Perhaps this realization will help us harness our desires for domination. Our purpose on earth is not to take responsibility from others who need the weight of their own responsibility in order to grow. We are here to encourage, to teach correct principles, to extend a helping hand, and to follow correct principles ourselves. We need to cautiously avoid the patterns of codependency that create an unhealthy feeling of responsibility for others, while neglecting our responsibility for and to ourselves.

There exists a delicate balance between helping too much and not helping enough, between allowing the world of natural consequences to take effect when people are destroying themselves and intervening in an effort to stop that destruction. When it comes to families, governments, legal systems, and social systems, finding that balance is a constant challenge. We must remember that God himself does not interfere with us even when we make choices that endanger our mental health or our very lives, or prevent us from coming back into his presence. This statement of Fritz Pearls expresses free agency quite well: "You do your thing and I'll do mine. I'm not here to live up to your expectations nor are you here to live up to mine."

Not License, But Responsibility

God has given us a map for the journey of life, but on this map there is not just one, but many successful paths that lead back to him—all of course paved with the same commandments, principles, and ordinances. None of us will return to God on exactly the same path, but with the access to inspiration and the good minds God has given us, we can find the path that will be successful to us. It is not uncommon to hear people say something like "I'm tired of having to make so many decisions, of having to think all the time, of having to guard my mouth and my actions." Thinking all the time and being courteous and conscientious are all part of self-mastery and they are qualities God would have us embrace. Using our free agency to learn to live the commandments is what it is all about. However, it isn't easy, and self-mastery doesn't come without a lot of patience and long-suffering. Still, it is one of our most important goals.

Self-mastery

What tho I conquer my enemies,
and lay up store and pelf,
I am a conqueror poor indeed,
Till I subdue myself.

What tho I read and learn by heart
Whole books while I am young,
I am a linguist in disgrace,

Who cannot guard my tongue.
What tho on campus I excel
A champ in meet and fight
If trained, efficient still I can't
Control an appetite.

What tho exemptions write my name
High on the honor-roll,
Electives, solids fail me if
I learn no self-control.

What tho I graduate and soar
And life is good to me,
My heart shall write me failure until
I learn SELF-MASTERY.
-Author Unknown-

Self-mastery is based on *choice* and comes only through our own efforts and through taking responsibility for our own choices. Many Church members want more than general guidance; they want absolutes. These members need to know that there can be no absolutes in such a private quest.

Choices Are Everything, and the Stakes Are High

Aleksandr Solzhenitsyn said,

> During the 300 years of Western civilization, there has been a sweeping away of duties and an expansion of rights. But we have two lungs. You can't breathe with just one lung and not the other. We must avail ourselves of rights and duties in equal measure. . . . The only thing we have been developing is rights, rights, rights, at the expense of duty.

The word "choose" has enormous power in it. It is a word nearly synonymous with responsibility and free agency. The word "can't," on the other hand, is debilitating and often a signal that someone is unwilling to take responsibility for their decisions. When people say, "This is what I choose to do," they acknowledge their control in the situation. When they say, "I can't stand it and there's nothing I can do about it," they do not acknowledge any power they might have, and they may be setting themselves up to play the victim role.

I once saw a man admitted to a psychiatric hospital because of severe depression. His wife had decided to leave him for another man. He complained that for several years she had been unhappy with him and had harassed him excessively about his lack of accomplishments. He was a professional man who had worked long hard hours and provided well for his family. When his wife ran off to fantasyland with another man, he basically said, "I can't stand it. I'd be better off dead." The man felt like a helpless victim. His divorce was inevitable; his wife refused any intervention and he had no control over what his wife chose to do. During counseling sessions with this man I got him to ask himself why he had chosen to remain in a relationship that was so negative. Why had he put up with the constant degradation from his spouse? "Are you a masochist?" I asked him. Eventually he realized that the experience he had been tolerating was unnecessary. With this realization he was able to become his own man and leave his wife emotionally. He decided that just as she had chosen to abuse him and leave him, he could choose to let her go and begin a new life.

Making this choice had two consequences. First, he started feeling better about himself. He no longer saw the divorce as a death equivalency, but as a decision he had helped make and with which he agreed. Secondly, his wife wondered about the source of his new-found strength. She questioned him about his counseling and eventually came in herself. Eventually they began communicating again. With his increase in self-respect, she too respected him more.

People are constantly telling me, "I would be happy if only George would do this . . . if my boss would do that . . . if my kids were like this . . ." But the challenge of life is for each of us to be responsible for our *own* lives—not to try to change other people's lives. With this awareness, we can choose to change our attitudes and our direction when the situation calls for it. The pattern of increasing awareness of our responsibility is graphically illustrated in the following piece:

Autobiography in Five Short Chapters

Chapter 1

I walk down the street.
There is a deep hole in the sidewalk.
I fall in . . . I am lost . . . I am helpless . . .
It isn't my fault.
It takes forever to find a way out.

Chapter 2

I walk down the same street.
There is a deep hole in the sidewalk.
I pretend I don't see it.
I fall in again. I can't believe I am in this same place.
But it isn't my fault. It still takes a long time to get out.

Chapter 3

I walk down the same street.
There is a deep hole in the sidewalk. I see it is there.
I still fall in . . . it's a habit . . . but my eyes are open.
I know where I am. It is my fault, my responsibility.
I get out immediately.

Chapter 4

I walk down the same street.
There is a deep hole in the sidewalk.
I walk around it.

Chapter 5

I walk down another street.

—Portia Nelson

SANITY STRATEGY #6

DISCOVER THE BUTTERFLY IN YOUR COCOON

Knowing yourself is the most important task to accomplish in the quest for mental health. When you know who you are and what you want, you may find that other relationships fall into place. It is important to be familiar with your beliefs and assumptions about yourself and to be actively engaged in nurturing these beliefs in directions you want to go in your life. When you uncover your core self and accept and nurture it, a more calm, stable, and secure self emerges. With the confidence and self-acceptance this brings, life then has purpose and happiness, while depression and hopelessness are kept at bay.

Because individuality is such an important component of self-esteem, I often make personalized tapes for my patients to help give them a sense of their uniqueness. The following is an example:

> I am John Doe, and I am unique and different. In all the billions of combinations of variables in the world, there is no one else like me. There may be a few people who have some parts like I do, but in the long run, no one really adds up exactly like I do. Therefore, I realize that everything which comes out of me is unique and authentic; it has rarity and exceptionality.
>
> Most important is the fact that I own me. I own my eyes, including all that they behold. I own my ears, including all the sounds and words they hear. I own my feelings, including all of my emotions—whether they be joy, love, anger, or excitement. I own my behaviors, whether they be toward me or toward others. I own my triumphs. I own my defeats.
>
> I know that as I go through this life, there will be some things I do not know about myself. But as long as I choose to be friendly

and accepting toward myself, I can have the courage to look at those things and make whatever changes are necessary.

However I look and sound, whatever I say and do, whatever I think or feel at some moment in time is me; when I review later how I looked and sounded, thought and did, I may decide that this is not right for me. But because I own me, I have the power to change or discard those things that are not right or good for me. Furthermore, I can replace them with new and creative ways of being. That which I have proven right and good, I can keep. As owner, I am engineer and architect of my own life. I realize more and more the importance of free agency and the power of choice. When God gave me the freedom of choice, He also gave the promise that if I used it with justice and creativity, I would be productive.

I can not only survive, I can make a difference. I realize that perfection is a process, just as life is. And as I begin to perceive life as a process and not just a destination, I learn to enjoy the journey more and to become more and more okay.

Only by discovering our own uniqueness can we fully appreciate the rewards of honest self-evaluation. The picture of ourselves that different people and institutions show us is merely a warped reflection, such as those from mirrors in the carnival of our modern society that picture us as taller, fatter, dumber, or less kind than we really are. But gaining an accurate perception of ourselves isn't as easy as looking in a mirror. We must be prepared to search and be tested. As members of the Church, we have some special help in this quest—patriarchal blessings and other blessings often give us a glimpse of the way the Lord sees us, which is the only totally accurate perception.

TRANSACTIONAL ANALYSIS

Transactional analysis (TA) provides a framework for self-evaluation. It is a useful tool for cataloging and evaluating our behaviors and feelings and for understanding the dynamics of our interactions with others and with ourselves. TA focuses on the interplay of internal dynamics (different ego states) within each of us.

The transactional approach to analysis says that there are different ego states within each person and that we should try to establish a balance between them. Ego states are not personalities, but rather a set of feelings, emotions, assumptions and conclusions. Each ego state has different feelings and thoughts, and they are often conscious of one another. The conflict between the different ego states is real and sometimes intense. When people say things such as "It seems like there is a battle going on inside of me," it may well be that they are experiencing conflict between their different ego states.

Knowing that people have different ego states and that each has its different orientations, preferences, fears, values, beliefs, and even behaviors is very helpful. Many people are unaware that the feelings of others may vary with ego states. Often, a patient will ask me something like "Is that how my wife (son, boss) really feels about me?" I usually say that, at that time and in that ego state, they probably do feel that way. This does not necessarily mean that they feel that way all the time—only in that ego state at that time.

To help us understand these ego dynamics, I think it would be important to look at the following illustration that identifies four key ego states: the critical parent, the nurturing parent, the child (rebellious and adaptive), and the integrated adult. The achievement of the integrated adult is the ultimate goal of the approach. That is, a logical, rational, objective adult integrated with the loving, caring, extending feelings of a nurturing parent and the fun and excitement of the free, spontaneous, curious child.

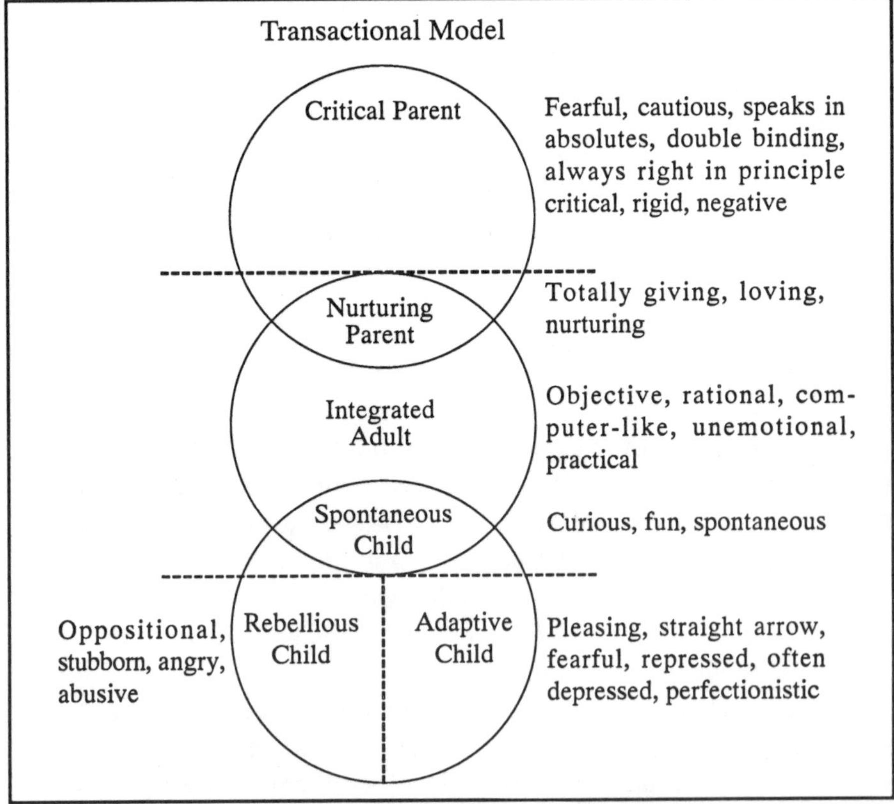

Now, let's look at some of the characteristics of these ego states. For the sake of clarity, I will refer to the ego states as *parent*, *child*, and *adult*. Let's begin with the parent.

The *parent* ego state in each of us likes to argue from principles. Since arguing from principles is considered an activity for the wise, the parent has the appearance of always being right. But being "right" can sometimes be both wrong and degrading to the child. The parent in us may say, "If you went to sacrament meeting with a better spirit, you'd get more out of the meetings." "If you read the scriptures more consistently, you'd understand the gospel more fully." "If you did your genealogy work, you would better understand temple work." All are true, but if our internal parent uses these truths as clubs to knock us down and beat us up, these comments become so overwhelming that we literally want to give up. Rather than being words of encouragement, they become demands that discourage us and produce rebellion and discouragement.

The critical parent state in us may also be double binding so that whatever we do is wrong. Let's use the example of seeing a professional counselor. The critical parent in us may say to the child in us, "Well, you've always been weak. You are the type of person who has always been dependent upon other people, and I guess weak people like you should see counselors." If you don't see a counselor, but you truly need help, the critical parent may say, "Well, you always have been stubborn; you've never taken advice from people, and you always reject help." Whatever choice we make, the parent inside us may have a tendency to be highly critical and double binding.

The critical parent may also make it impossible for us to accept praise of any kind. When we are stroked in any way, the critical parent inside us may discount the praise. This, of course, has a great impact on interpersonal relationships because other people may tire of having their compliments discredited.

Conversely, in some cases a critical parent ego state may harrass the child ego not into isolation but into dependency. This happens when there is constant criticism from the parent ego state that leads a person to seek nurturing from others in an extreme, compulsive, or unhealthy way as a means of compensation.

However, if the nurturing parent ego state in us can take over some of the nurturing, this dependency on others can be avoided. The nurturing parent is loving, kind, and accepting; it gives unconditional love. This may sound wonderful, but balance is essential because the overactive nurturing parent ego has a tendency to care for others at the expense of self. If your nurturing parent becomes dominant, then you will be easily exploited, and may wear yourself to a frazzle, yet still feel you can never do enough for other people. (This is undoubtedly one of the factors that contributes to codependency.) So acting from the position of nurturing parent without the balance of logic and reason from the adult becomes a personal weakness.

I know of one widow, for instance, who spent her entire life's savings in legal battles to rescue her son from prison even though he was a confirmed criminal. This woman's nurturing parent was so much in control of her that she was unable to face reality and overcome her need to come to his rescue. The nurturing parent is typically pushed into the area of unhealthy excess by guilt and over-indulgence, which can, in turn, make children self-indulgent. I recently saw an example of this when a mother found it necessary to admit her teenage son to the psychiatric ward of the hospital. Her son was completely out of control. He ran up and down the corridors of the ward calling his mother names and kicking doors. Instead of leaving as was suggested so the doctors would be better able to calm the boy down, the mother stayed, apologizing again and again to her son for admitting him. When the woman finally left the boy did calm down. This mother was so consumed with guilt fed by her out-of-balance nurturing parent state that she could not react rationally. Clearly then, there are dangers in the potentially good "nurturing parent" ego-state if it is not integrated with the logic of the "adult" ego state.

On the other hand, if the critical parent ego state becomes dominant, we may often hear critical parent messages such as "Negative feelings must be suppressed and forgotten," "The body and its functions are dirty," and "You should only think of others—not yourself."

Since the critical parent ego-state is so adept at making the child feel oppressed and inferior, many people want to attack the parent ego-state and try to drive it out of their heads. Instead, what we need to do is let the integrated adult ego intervene as much as possible, without threatening the critical parent ego. The critical parent ego state is like a mother bear in the woods. If we get between her and her cubs, she will tear us apart. Likewise, the critical parent ego-state, if threatened with annihilation, will attack ferociously.

I often see therapists trying to get the child or the adult ego states to attack the critical parent ego state and say, "You get out of my life. I will have nothing to do with you." While this may sound good on the surface, eventually the parent ego will come back in stronger and more subtle ways. Any parent realizes that there is no job more overwhelming, or one that can make one feel quite as inadequate, as parenting. If we add to a parent's fear of inadequacy with threats, accusations, or alienation, that parent will usually retaliate. So will the parent ego-state. The parent ego-state in a patient, when threatened, will sabotage all therapeutic efforts, whether overt on the part of the therapist or covert on the part of the patient. We must quietly reassure the parent ego—by establishing and clarifying good values using solid reasoning and working out of a model of respect—that we fully accept the principles this parent ego-state believes. That part of our mind is actually very important to us. When fed with true and proper data, it can be an important part of our conscience. The parent ego tries to do the best it can to keep us on the "right" path. Problems arise because, as discussed in Chapter 1, many of the guidelines we have fed into our parent ego computers are based on traditions, opinions, and personal preferences that do not fit our personal needs and may hinder our progress. Our integrated adult ego-state, having the ability to reason this out and discard unhelpful beliefs, can assist the parent ego in its responsibilities, but cannot assume those responsibilities by "getting rid of" the parent ego.

As indicated, the child is actually two ego states. First, there is the adaptive child who cannot do enough to comply and continually tries to adapt to all wishes of the critical parent. This child in us continually, but passively, incorporates all of the problems, guilt, and frustrations of the parent ego-state. The child therefore placates by acknowledging and expressing guilt; but after the child ego-state has grovelled in guilt long enough, and the parent still does not let up, the child ego-state may motivate withdrawal, despair, depression, and even suicidal thoughts. Understanding this concept can give us further motivation to examine our beliefs, and weed out unrealistic expectations, perfectionism, and other false beliefs that contribute to this depressing cycle.

The second child ego-state (the rebellious child) crops up after the adaptive child ego-state has tried to please or placate the parent ego-state and failed. This rebellious period usually leads the parent ego-state to strongly reassert itself; renewed guilt is the predictable result. The cycle continues, of course, with more rebellion manifested in tantrums, passive–aggressive behaviors, conduct disorder, substance abuse, or suicide. The overt destructiveness of the final possibility, suicide, is symbolic of the destructiveness of the other stages of this kind of rebellion. Victories in these wars are purely Pyrrhic ("victory at any price") where, really, everybody loses.

Any of these ego-states can be a problem if carried to extremes—

we need to have the balance made possible only through the integrated adult state.

In order to better understand the inner workings of these different states, I have created an illustration that considers four issues seen from each of the ego-states.

Issue 1: Seeing a Therapist

Critical Parent	Adaptive or Rebellious Child	Integrated Adult
You are sick and must see someone. You have always been weak and dependent. or So now you won't go! You really are stubborn.	I'd better go and see someone because I'm so weak. or Leave me alone! I hate the way you always try to make me the sick one.	Seeing a psychologist may help. I will look into the cost and availability of good professional help.

Issue 2: Going to Church

Critical Parent	Adaptive or Rebellious Child	Integrated Adult
If you don't go to church, you will disappoint God and disgrace the family. God will not love you if you don't go. or You better go so you don't have anything bad happen to you.	If I don't go, I will not get any privileges: no car, no friends, etc. or You make me hate the Church. I will only hate it, and you can't make me like it.	A few hours a week is a small price to pay to have peace in my life.

Issue 3: Taking Medications

Critical Parent	Adaptive or Rebellious Child	Integrated Adult
Because you are weak and defective you have to take medicines. or I don't know why you have to rely on medicines. I guess you always have been weak.	I better take my medicine because I am sick and weak. or No one is going to poison me. You just want to control me!	It is practical at this time to take medicine—my doctor believes it best, and I am seeking his advice and opinion.

Issue 4: Buying a Car

Critical Parent	Adaptive or Rebellious Child	Integrated Adult
You want to buy a new car? Are you crazy? The depreciation, payments, and insurance will put you in the poor house. or You're going to buy a used car? You really are dumb to buy someone else's headaches.	I really can't afford to make a mistake. What if I lose my job or choose the wrong car? or I'll buy what I want. You have no right to tell me what to do.	I will weigh prices, insurance, financing, and warranties against my income and needs and then make the best decision I can.

The goal, as I see it, is to function as much of the time as possible in the integrated adult ego-state. That is, to be a rational, objective, integrated adult with the good feelings of the loving, giving, nurturing parent and the fun, curious, free child combined. It is important to recognize that the free child and the nurturing parent traits are vital to the balance of the personality. Without them the adult ego state is boring because it is void of feelings and emotions. The pure adult only looks at life in an objective, logical, rational way. Granted, if all we had was a nurturing side to us, or a fun, free-spirited side with no logic and objectivity as a balance, we would get into trouble quickly. The goal would be to minimize the negative dynamics between the critical parent and the rebellious or adaptive child through the increased activity and involvement of the integrated adult ego-state.

Sally, a married woman in her late thirties, came to see me with numerous complaints. Besides depressive complaints and complaints of confusion about what she should do and be in life, she had many physical complaints. In an attempt to correct her physical complaints she had undergone several surgeries, mainly in the abdominal area. After her surgeries, however, her pains remained and seemed to become even more mystical and hard to define. When the doctors could find no physical reason for her pain, they concluded she had a somatization disorder. Such people have unresolved conflicts which they tend to internalize; consequently, their anxieties, worries, and fears manifest themselves physiologically.

Some of the faulty critical parent messages Sally was receiving from her past experiences were, "I have to do well in school," "I can't stand it when my house is messy," "What will people think of me if . . . ?", and "People always get what they deserve."

Further, her parent ego messages were reflective of some of the hyper-regulating sayings and opinions that are sometimes put forth in church meetings as doctrines. Rather than being uplifting and encouraging, they only caused her to ruminate, brood, and feel inadequate. Then she began putting perfectionistic demands on herself, which led her to see herself as the total contrast to "The glory of God is intelligence," "Cleanliness is next to godliness," and "Be ye therefore perfect even as your Father which is in Heaven is perfect." Even uplifting scriptures were used, not as inspiration and encouragement, but as clubs and putdowns.

Sally's reactive child responses were "I'll never make it." "I wish I were as good as other people." "Why can't I get more done?" "I don't deserve my blessings." It took time for Sally to confront her parent ego and relieve her child ego from some of the heavy burdens placed on it. Some of the commandments, rules, and beliefs located in her parent and child egos were so integrated into her personality system that they had become "sacred cows."

When Sally was finally able to redefine her life circumstances in more integrated adult terms, her symptoms began to lift. As she was able to rewrite many of her commandments, seeing them more realistically and accepting them in a more adult and rational way, she began to do much better in her marriage, social life, and family life.

She began to change ideas like, "Anything worth doing is worth doing well" to statements like, "Some things are worth doing well, some things are only worth doing, and some things aren't worth doing at all," and she came to a much happier balance in her life.

Sally had been trying to go back to college but was so perfectionistic that she would drop out of her classes periodically, fearing that she couldn't possibly get an A grade. Usually she dropped out in mid-semester, using minor health problems and family situations that she could interpret as crises as her excuses.

When she realized that it would be better to pass a course with a B than to drop the class and have nothing to show for her work, her inner pressures seemed to subside.

When Sally also came to terms with the idea that it was better to clean her house some than not to clean it at all, she began to feel more efficient. Another breakthrough was the realization that she didn't have to compare herself with others but only with herself. This relieved the competition within her own mind.

In short, not only did Sally's physical symptoms subside, but she became a more pleasant person to be around. Her humor increased, she began to smile more, and her overall manner and appearance seemed much less stern and rigid.

The transactional model (TA) provides a convincing case for the importance of a healthy self-respect. Most people who are struggling are experiencing the negative and often subtle dynamics between the critical adult and the child. They have never really evaluated their own set of values and beliefs. They react like adaptive or rebellious children who are reacting to the values, principles, rules, and laws imposed by critical parents but never analyzed by themselves. Without respect for ourselves based on living in harmony with our own carefully thought out values and beliefs, we are doomed to a life of vulnerability, hopelessness, anger, and resentment.

Shortly after her marriage to a man she adored, Jill found herself in great conflict. Seeking counseling, she was taught of these different ego states and became able to recognize that her critical parent was unrelenting in its criticism of the man she chose, while her child was wildly excited and thrilled with him. While he mirrored many of the characteristics she herself valued, such as, honesty, openness, and capacity to love, he did not conform to the letter of the law "checklist" she had been taught to look for and value. She was motivated to sort out the differences between her own values and preferences and those imposed on her. Respect for her own right to choose and to prioritize values made it possible for her to calm the battle she had been engaged in and reassure her critical parent state that she was not turning her back on primary values.

Self-Respect Model

A TA model can help us catalog, and therefore evaluate, how we act, think, and feel so that we can function from an integrated adult ego state more and more of the time. Ultimately though, we need to develop a self-respect model that allows us to do this.

"Know the truth and the truth shall make you free" is commonly taught. Self-respect and esteem should be firmly rooted in our quest for truth, not based on misunderstandings, misconceptions, distortions, falsities, or upon some of the distorted, fanciful misconceptions we oftentimes hold to tenaciously. Self-respect and esteem are not directly measurable and should not be considered in direct analytical terms. Rather, they come from the firm, quiet, acceptance, understanding, and independence of what one represents in reality.

In my experience, people with true self-respect adhere to a personal and purposeful set of goals and values that is rooted in truth. Just as importantly, the individual is willing to work, sacrifice (suffer, endure, delay gratification, commit efforts), and uphold the demands of that set of values and goals.

These people are so committed and zealous that they do not focus on and complain about sacrifice. While history is full of dramatizations of people who have fully given their lives—all around us we have those who quietly go about the Lord's business with extreme dedication and without regard to how others may view their behaviors. Such dedication is reflected in the eighty-six-year-old man who is at the Church missionary headquarters arguing that he should be able to go on a mission and is willing to arm wrestle anyone who would try to deny him that privilege. Others in their elderly years are getting up at 2:30 a.m. to go to the temple and prepare for the early arriving patrons. When people truly have self-esteem and respect, they enjoy purpose, meaning, balance, hope, and self-acceptance.

Sanity Strategy #7

Get to Know What Is and What Isn't

Sometimes our perceptions of ourselves are not reality-based. This makes self-evaluation an enormous challenge. The challenge can be even more complicated if we use the New Testament measuring stick—perfection—which seems so damning to us. However, when we judge ourselves according to a model of self-respect that we gain through maturity, understanding, prayer, and commitment to a reality based value system, we begin to love ourselves more.

When we read of Jesus saying, "Be ye, therefore perfect even as your Father which is in heaven is perfect" (Matt. 5:48) we need to remember that our Father in Heaven *became* perfect. The footnote in the new scriptures tells us that perfect means "finished, complete, fully developed." Perfection didn't happen all at once for him and it won't for us. Perfection is a long step-by-step process never finished in mortality.

Mental health and happiness is contingent to a great degree upon self-esteem, and self-esteem is a function of accurate self-evaluation with which we can develop a healthy self-respect.

I see many patients who are alienated from themselves. The difference between what a person would like to be and what he perceives himself to be is a fairly reliable indicator of his level of dissatisfaction with himself. While not many people ever measure up to their ego ideal, we cannot cope if we are too far removed from it. Of course, some people's ego ideals are set much too high. They need to take an honest look at their efforts and abilities and realize that if they continue to strive for the unreachable, they will suffer dangerous consequences.

We should be careful not to define ourselves negatively. Too many of us discredit and devalue ourselves. We need to realize that we do have exceptionality and rarity that corresponds to our unique missions and responsibilities here on this earth.

An important aspect of self-esteem is how we think others see us. Nearly everybody wants other people to like them and approve of them. As long as this is only a general desire, it may be acceptable. But when we decide that it is a dire necessity or an absolute need to have everyone's approval all of the time, we have set ourselves up for a lot of pain and suffering because that is an impossible goal—there will always be people that tend to be critical of us.

Think through how much of your core self-respect is built upon how others see you. If your self-respect "model" double-binds or negates you, it may well be based on an untruth—something you simply grew up with and internalized, perhaps an opinion or statement imposed upon you by teachers or parents. For example, they may have told you that you had "two left feet," and you accepted it as reality because of your lack of experience in judging your own abilities. Such judgments may even have been true at the time, but because you believed them they may, unless they are challenged, become part of your self-image for a lifetime.

It is not uncommon for people to experience wide swings in self-esteem levels depending upon their situation. A brain surgeon may feel great about himself only when he's doing brain surgery. Other people are on top of the world while they are involved in the annual charity drive but feel lousy the other fifty-one weeks of the year. A healthy model of self-respect is consistent, not dependent on our performance or other's opinions. It helps us feel good toward ourselves even when we have made mistakes or are not performing at our best. A well-rounded view of ourselves can contribute to positive mental health.

Good mental health requires us to ultimately live out of our own model of respect. Many people are too busy trying to please everyone else by trying to be what others want them to be. It is good to have role models and to accept encouragement, but if we are merely chameleons we will end up unhappy and depressed. We cannot, ultimately, make everyone happy. Our first responsibility is to ourselves.

We need to realize that a "model of self-respect" is more than the sum of its parts. It really comes down to good feelings regarding a set of criteria, values, and beliefs. Its key component is a feeling that "I am going in the right direction. I am becoming okay, and the feeling that I am okay is coming from within me, not from others."

Reality Testing

Probably the biggest goal of mental health is to help people do what we call reality testing. As the term implies this is making sure that our assumptions and judgements square with reality.

Our assumptions and interpretations, positive or negative, are contingent upon numerous factors: self-esteem, prejudices, attitudes, and orientations. A major part of my job as a therapist is assisting people in defining their realities differently, or at least more accurately. Stephan J. Hall said, "Your judgement and interpretation are only as good as your information." Many psychiatric and personality disorders reflect inadequate information and reality testing difficulties.

For example, someone you know fairly well comes walking down the aisle in a store and passes you. This person looks straight at you but doesn't acknowledge your existence. You would probably find that behavior insulting and confusing. It is easy to observe behavior, but it is sometimes difficult to interpret it. Most of us would jump immediately to one conclusion or another, but we all know that jumping to conclusions, or making hasty assumptions, often gets people into a great deal of trouble. Let's take the case in point, analyze what we observed, and make some possible interpretations. Let's say the person who passed you is also the bishop. Here are some possible interpretations:

1. The bishop is an insensitive person and doesn't care for me.
2. I am a person not worth being considered.
3. The bishop is having a bad day and isn't aware of his surroundings.
4. The bishop is embarrassed to be around me.
5. The bishop is aware of my sinful state and therefore won't recognize me.
6. The bishop is ignoring me because he knows something is wrong with my family.
7. The bishop is preoccupied with something.

Which of these is true? It is too early to tell, and it is inappropriate for us to come to any conclusions until we have more information. Hasty conclusions can be devastating both to the people who are judged inappropriately and to the person who is making that judgement. Many of these incorrect assumptions are made by people who have a tendency toward negativism, guilt, or self-doubt; these people project these feelings onto other people, quickly drawing conclusions about a situation that are often wildly inaccurate.

For example, a man who I once counseled managed a branch of a major bank. At the first of the year, when salary increases were given out, this man discovered that he had received only a 5% raise in salary. He had been expecting much more. Since he took over this particular branch three years ago, it had far exceeded the other branches statistically. There had been fewer losses, better loans, and more profit. He felt as though his good works had essentially gone unrecognized, and he was disappointed and angry. His interpretations of the situation was "Nobody reads the statistical reports. Doing a good job doesn't count. Salaries must be prone to politics."

I told him that I couldn't tell whether his interpretations were correct. I did not have the information, but I encouraged him to write down his thoughts, go to one of the head vice-presidents of the bank and, in a tactful manner, tell him of his observations, and interpretations. I reminded him to follow the guidelines for effective problem solving—to use "I" messages, not to raise his voice, and so forth. This man finally took courage and approached one of the vice-presidents.

During the interview he learned that the bank had not done very well that year and that a 5% raise was much better than any other manager in the company had received. Some of the other managers had even lost their company cars. When this man came out of the interview, his situation had not changed—he still would receive only a 5% raise—but his definition of reality, and thus his feelings, had changed dramatically. Although nothing had changed except his understanding of the facts, he no longer felt angry or unrewarded.

To enhance reality testing, I try to get people to take their impression of themselves and look at it from four different perspectives. I use four different adjective lists that represent their four different selves to accomplish this (see adjective list at the back of the book). First, I have them fill out one adjective checklist that they feel represents their real self—the person they perceive themselves to be. Next they choose adjectives they feel represents their ideal self—the person they would like to become. Next, I have them select the adjectives that depict the feared self—the person they are afraid they could become. Fourth, they choose adjectives for their perception of the presented self—the self they present to the world.

Many patients have a lot of difficulty with this last self. We might call this the mask, the image we allow the world to see.

Sometimes to help them with this self, I ask them to get several people who know them to also fill out the checklist.

Interestingly, most of the acquaintances' evaluations are fairly consistent. Once all the checklists are completed on the different selves, we sit down and look at them. If the person is depressed, it is interesting to note that their real self, that is, the person they see themselves as being, and the person others describe, are usually very different. Most of the adjectives under the real self are much more negative than the presented self.

Many people, especially those in a depressed state, have trouble discounting the negative comments of other people, even if those evaluations are extremely isolated. I ask them to imagine conducting a survey of thirty-one people on how well they liked a new restaurant. We have these people grade the service, food, and atmosphere of the restaurant on a scale from zero to five.

Suppose thirty of the people circled all fours and fives, implying that all three areas were either very good or excellent. However, one person circled all zeros indicating poor or very poor. How would we write up the findings? Generally speaking, we would tell the restaurant owners they are doing a good job. We may not even include the one interview, or we might discount it heavily because a sample of one is simply not very meaningful. We should do the same thing with the negative comments of other people.

Impaired reality testing can have devastating results. I remember one situation where the parents of a young missionary received word that their son was on his way home under dishonorable circumstances. He had been excommunicated. The parents went to the ticket counter at the airport and left some cash in an envelope and a note telling him they could not bear to see him. They added they would rather have had him come home dead than have him come back under these conditions. They saw the situation as much worse than it really was. Their inability to recognize that their son had only made a mistake and that he needed their help, not their condemnation, resulted in much more tragic consequences. This young man eventually took his own life.

Mentally healthy people can, by continuously gathering information, test the validity of their judgments and assumptions. Mental health professionals are trained to help those people who, for one reason or another, have become unable to discern when their own perceptions do not match reality. Their assumptions, however faulty, may have become their reality and have caused difficulties in their lives, which if left unchecked become a souce of great unhappiness.

One mistake some people make is to compare their reality to a fantasy. Fantasies are perfect; reality cannot compete with them. Therefore, it is a mistake to compare your life with the life of a heroine in a soap opera or to compare your spouse or children with the fantastic people in magazine photos and romance novels. By doing so we are making false assumptions about what is going on in our world. Remember, it is easy to observe behavior but more difficult to interpret it and respond appropriately.

Value Clarification and Goal Setting

Another method used to analyze and to provide a foundation for self-respect and self-esteem is called value clarification. A value, as contrasted with a goal, is broad and not directly measurable. Some things may always be of value, but they may increase or decrease in priority with age or situation. For example, health is always a value, but you are likely to emphasize it much more if you have just been diagnosed with cancer or a major heart problem. Financial security may always be a value, but it seems more critical at age sixty than at twenty-two.

Viktor Frankl, a noted psychiatrist imprisoned in the Nazi prison camps in Germany during WWII, wanted to understand why some people gave up and died while others lived when faced with the same terrible circumstances. He concluded that the survivors lived because they had a sense of purpose and retained their values.

Frankl wrote a book about his conclusions called *Man's Search for Meaning*. He wrote of four major values he discovered in the lives of those who survived: (l) a sense of lifework or purpose they were living to fulfill, (2) a powerful love of family whom they believed they would see in the future, (3) a sense of patriotism and the importance of freedom, and (4) a profound belief in God. By being in touch with the spiritual, their belief in their survival was enhanced.

It is interesting to note that these four values are tied very closely to goals. Because of this, I suggest you try a value clarification exercise that leads directly to effective goal setting. It is not a quick, five-minute project. The key to this exercise is detail and specificity.

If you approached a building contractor about building your house, you would probably already have ideas about what your priorities were in the construction of the home—you could probably rate the relative intensity of your concerns about maintenance, economy, utility, flexibility, spaciousness, and attractiveness. Similarly, if we clarify our personal values we can resolve feelings that stem from confused values. As with house plans, the more specific we are the easier it is to plan how to get what we desire.

It is wise to delay goal-setting and planning until we have our values defined, understood and ranked. Ask yourself: "What kind of life do I want to build?" In other words, what is the fundamental orientation or foundation on which you are building? The purpose of value clarification is to define and clarify what we are trying to build. Once the format of values is laid out and prioritized (i.e., the activities we want to engage in, the people we want to associate with), the long-term goals can be put in place.

First, write down those things that you value and then rank them by priority. Although the order in which we rank them varies dramatically, some examples that appear on many of our lists will be:

mental health	financial security
spiritual health	leisure activities
physical health	immediate family
marriage	extended family
parenthood	neighbors

You may also want to list specific personality attributes such as patience or tolerance.

Next, list in column form the people, places, things, and activities that "enhance" these values and make them attainable. Just as different elements of a well-built house tend to support each other, primary values actually enhance other values. For instance, many people value an open and friendly disposition for its own sake, and yet this open and friendly disposition naturally results in professional benefits because people like them. This in turn increases their success and contributes to their financial security. The result of balanced primary values is an integrated, supportive value structure within the individual.

Finally, once you have listed your core values and the things that enhance them, *measurable* goals, both short and long term, can be set. If these goals are rooted in a strong value system, you will find them more meaningful and be more committed to attaining them.

Any number of activities may enhance a particular value. But just as we emphasize core values differently, we may also favor dramatically different combinations of value enhancements. This exercise can help provide direction in your life precisely because it shows how our goals can be rooted in the value systems that are paramount to us. What follows is my own outline of enhancements and goals for one of my values: physical health.

Enhancement	Short-term Goal	Long term Goal
1. Word of Wisdom 2. Proper weight and rest 3. Recreation (tennis, hunting) 4. Mental health 5. Spirituality	1. Lose 10 lbs. this month. 2. Reduce red meat in diet to 1 time per week. 3. Go to exercise club 3 times per week. 4. Play tennis 3 times per week with Stan.	1. Weigh 215 lbs. by January. 2. Exercise 3 hours per week. 3. Play in tournament within the year.

Some examples of values which may be important to you are:

Love of Family	Health
Love of God	Integrity
Love of Country	Responsibility
Friendship	Creativity
Financial Security	Marriage
Service	Honesty
Generosity	Spirituality
Being a good parent	Enjoyable work

Select the ones that fit you, then add to these any others that you can think of that are meaningful, and then rank them according to their importance to you.

It is essential at this point to note that a goal which is an enhancement to one person's value may not enhance that same value for another person. For example, financial security may be valued equally by two different people, but one may see the goal of education as the key to enhancement, while the second chooses to stockpile gold. Reading the scriptures may enhance one person's spirituality, while another finds listening to speeches by general authorities more helpful.

Note also that one goal could enhance several values, thereby making the goal more important. A goal to lose weight, for instance, will enhance the value of physical health, but it will also enhance a person's self-esteem, social life, and perhaps even his spiritual life.

The importance of clarifying our governing values is obvious. After we have done this, we are ready for the goal-setting process.

Goal Setting

In setting goals there are some key points to keep in mind:

1. A goal should be written down, first in pencil, then later in ink. This crystallizes your thinking and intentions.
2. Make the goal specific and measurable. Unless you can tell when you have reached your goal, it is not really a goal, only a wish.
3. Determine whether you will need the support of others. Identify the people, groups, and organizations whose cooperation and assistance you will need to attain the goal. Then determine what you can give, how you can serve, contribute, or compensate others in order to obtain the help you need.
4. Determine the values that will be enhanced by the goal. If it enhances several major values, it is almost certainly the Lord's will for you—which is the most important bottom line for any goal.
5. Get a clear mental image of your goal as if it has already been attained. Play that picture on the screen of your mind every time you get a chance.
6. Determine what knowledge is needed to reach your goal, and how you will go about obtaining it.
7. Identify the obstacles you will have to overcome. Write them down. They usually appear larger than life unless they are on paper.
8. Believe you have the ability to achieve the goal.
9. Rate your commitment to the goal. On a scale of 1 to 10, how committed are you to the goal? If you can't honestly rate your commitment at 8 or better, rewrite the goal to one you honestly feel you have the ability and commitment to achieve.
10. Break down your goal into bite-sized pieces and tasks.
11. Plan your days to include the tasks you need to do to reach your goal.

The challenge is to set goals that are consistent with your value structure, because you gain power to reach goals when your actions are consistent with your values. That assurance clears you to confidently ask for the Lord's help. Therefore, make sure that each goal you set is based on a value you hold.

Goals are critical to most successful people, but many of us fail to make sure we are fully committed to our goals and that our goals are firmly rooted in a framework of solid value structures. In order for a value structure to be solid, it has to be something we are willing to dedicate ourselves to, suffer for, sacrifice for, and believe in absolutely. With true commitment to a good value system, nobody can rock us. No amount of ridicule or disagreement or questioning by others will have any negative effect on us, and we will be in a position to set meaningful goals, all based on these values.

The goal-setting procedure takes time and work, but it is a powerful tool to give your life more direction. You may wish to try the following: take three sheets of paper (or get a goal notebook). Head the first sheet: "My Lifetime Values and Goals." Write down all the things you would like to do, learn, be, acquire, or experience in your life. At this point, don't be concerned with what looks possible; think in terms of what you would really like if *anything* were possible. What would make your life worth living? Write down everything that comes to your mind.

On another sheet headed "My Five-Year Goals," choose from the first list those things that you most want to accomplish, experience, learn, and acquire over the next five years. Again, go for quantity.

On a third page headed, "My Six-Month Goals," list all the things you would do if you had only six months to live. How would you live your last six months of life on earth? Now, look at all three lists. Do the five-year goals build toward your lifetime goals? How about the six-month goals? Did your other two lists coordinate with that list? Are you directing your energy toward your most important goals at this point in your life? If not, what do you need to change?

Setting goals consistent with our values and thinking about them and working on them continuously, raises our self-image and moves us toward the integrated adult state—toward peak performance and full realization of our potential. Then why do so many of us avoid setting goals?

There are seven major reasons:

1. We may not understand the importance of values and goals.
2. We may not know how to commit to values and set goals.
3. We may have a fear of commitment.
4. We may have a fear of change.
5. We may have a fear of failure.
6. We may even have a fear of success.
7. Finally, the "natural man" is just flatout lazy. We may have to confront our inclination to take the path of least resistance. Be mindful that entropy and laziness are probably the biggest evils we commonly confront.

Are any of these roadblocks to success holding you back? Writing your goals and following the steps I have outlined can help you take control of your life and change dreams into reality.

SANITY STRATEGY #8

Remodel Your Mind with Joy Principles

When the Ten Commandments were given to Moses, I believe they were purposely made very short. Nevertheless, these simple commandments trigger complex emotions and ideas. It only takes a few moments to read the Ten Commandments, but the amount of thought that they produce is both extensive and provocative. Learning to live them completely may take a lifetime but is worthy of every effort. The same is true of the ten principles we will discuss in this chapter.

Principle #1
Perfection Is a Process Not a Status

Another way to spell perfectionism in normal living is P-A-R-A-L-Y-S-I-S. If we feel that we have to do everything in a perfect way, we will eventually become immobilized. "I'm not going to do this until I can do it perfectly" is a prescription for paralysis. Perfection is an unrealistic expectation in mortality. A realistic expectation is doing "our current best" and feeling satisfied with it.

Some of us need to realize that there are many arenas of life where excellence is simply not required. Relaxation of unrealistically high standards will always help us feel better about our performance.

Unfortunately, many feel adulthood itself demands perfection. They become overwhelmed with its perceived responsibilities. Those suffering from withdrawal, anorexia, or bulimia may be trying to revert back to the status of a child. Women may become emaciated to the point where the menses cease and breasts and other secondary sexual characteristics disappear. Not surprisingly, these women often hope to avoid the pressures and responsibilities of adulthood, especially the sexual ones. Simply put, they just want to be little girls again, unencumbered by adult problems and responsibilities.

Mature adults may also normally experience the urge to flee adulthood and its responsibilities. But while the gravity of one's commitments truly seem overwhelming, it is much more difficult for those who think their every step must be perfect. This paralysis is unfortunate because adult competence is, like all other properly internalized systems, learned step by step, precept upon precept.

Perfectionism can be used as an excuse for not trying. Many years ago, a friend of mine said if he could not get his Ph.D from one of the big name schools, he would not get it at all. Although he sounded like he had high ideals, his decision really appeared to be an attempt to avoid making the difficult decision to go through four more years of graduate work.

I want to emphasize the step-by-step nature of personal growth. Keeping in mind the law of eternal progression is quite helpful. We strive to be perfect, but we are not. Perfection is an eternal process that will continue even in the life hereafter.

The "Sisyphus Complex" is a classical example of the fear of personal growth becoming a form of paralysis. In Greek mythology, Sisyphus was cursed by Zeus to roll a large boulder to the top of a hill. But always, just as he neared the crest of the hill with his burden, swarms of devilish Gyhlors would bite and poke at his legs until he turned to kick them away. At this point, the boulder would roll down the hill, and Sisyphus, after some rest, would begin again. This was his eternal damnation.

I cannot tell you how many times I have met people who say that their goal for therapy is "to be thin" or "to be active in the Church" or "to have a temple marriage" or "to gain an administrative position in my company." However, these people—once they get going—consciously or unconsciously sabotage their own efforts. I can only conclude that in spite of their goals, these people are afraid of getting their burdens over the top of the hill, afraid of success.

One of the Gyhlors that stops the progress of many people who are afraid of success is the way they think and talk about what they are doing. It is easy to talk ourselves out of progress or success with quite ordinary language. Spoken words and thoughts can be powerful motivators or powerful impediments to our efforts.

We may find ourselves saying things like "That's going to be too hard." "I can't do that." "You don't understand how difficult this problem is for me." "That would be scary." "That's easier said than done."

Predictably, people don't like to be confronted with the possibility that they sabotage their own goals. They are unwilling to believe that they may have a will to fail. On occasion, I try to provoke people with exchanges like the following:

"Do you really want to lose weight?"

"Of course I do."

"Well, write down all the pros and cons of losing weight."

"Cons of losing weight?" they may question.

"There could be many," I reply. "People would make comments about your weight loss. You may have to deal with wolf whistles and sexual advances. You may be asked to engage in more social or sporting events. Could you stand this attention?"

For some, the answer is clearly "no" or "not yet." My job is to get them to realize this and to deal with it.

One of the things we can do is to change our attitudes and thoughts about any situation and change the way we talk to ourselves. We can change our negative self-talk to positive, even if we don't believe the statements at first. Two good self-talk statements are "This may be hard, but I can do it. I am not afraid of hard tasks" and "Perhaps that will be scary, but I've done scary things before, and once I have tried it I won't be afraid anymore."

In all these situations, the real question becomes, "Will I let my fears of failure or of self-improvement paralyze me into inaction? Or will I remember that perfection is a process, not a status?"

The process of perfecting ourselves is arduous but the rewards incomprehensible. Latter-day Saints understand that the goal of mortal existence is to return to our creator and gain exaltation—a state where man, quite literally, takes on the responsibilities and powers of godhood. As Joseph Fielding Smith said, "The Father has promised through the Son that all that he has shall be given to those who are obedient to his commandments. They shall increase in knowledge, wisdom, and power, going from grace to grace, until the fullness of the perfect day shall burst upon them." (*Doctrines of Salvation* 2:36.) I make this point for a reason. Some people feel passionately that the joy in mountaineering is the climb itself and that the summit is merely a cold and windy place. I consider that a healthy attitude for many situations in mortality, but for eternity it does not sit well with my spiritual convictions. I not only cherish the journey but look also to the summit which, to the Latter-day Saints, is godhood. Scott Peck's book, *The Road Less Traveled*, contains a moving explanation of the natural consequences of having a loving creator:

> "If we postulate that our capacity to love, this urge to grow and evolve, is somehow "breathed into" us by God, then we must ask to what end. Why does God want us to grow? What are we growing toward? What is it that God wants of us . . . for no matter how much we may like to pussyfoot around it, all of us who postulate a loving God and really think about it eventually come to a single terrifying idea: God wants us to become like Himself. . . . We are growing toward godhood. . . .
>
> Were we to believe it possible for man to become God, this belief by its very nature would place upon us an obligation to attempt to attain the possible. But we do not want this obligation. We don't want to have to work that hard. We don't want God's responsibility. We don't want the responsibility of having to think all the time. As long as we can believe that godhood is an impossible attainment for ourselves, we don't have to worry about our spiritual growth, we don't have to push ourselves to higher and higher levels of consciousness and loving activity; we can relax and just be human.
>
> If God's in his heaven and we're down here, and never the twain shall meet, we can let Him have all the responsibility for evolution and the directorship of the universe. We can do our bit toward assuring ourselves a comfortable old age, hopefully complete with healthy, happy and grateful children and grandchildren; but beyond that we need not bother ourselves.
>
> These goals are difficult enough to achieve, and hardly to be disparaged. Nonetheless, as soon as we believe it is possible for man to become God, we can really never rest for long, never say, "OK, my job is finished, my work is done." We must constantly push ourselves to greater and greater wisdom, greater and greater effectiveness. By this belief we will have trapped ourselves, at least until death, on a treadmill of self-improvement and spiritual growth. God's responsibility must be our own. It is no wonder that the belief in the possibility of Godhead is repugnant. The idea that God is actively nurturing us so that we might grow up to be like Him brings us face to face with our own laziness."

The plan of salvation is enormously challenging, but when God said, "Be ye therefore perfect, even as your Father which is in heaven is perfect," we must remember that God *became* perfect. He hopes we will do the same, but we must be patient with ourselves as He is patient with us. Hard work and honest self-appraisal will help us prepare to accept the process of repentance and the act of atonement, for they are the way of progress and eventually, perfection.

Principle #2
Don't Devalue or Discredit by Comparisons

The parable of the talents suggests strongly that Christ will judge people according to how well they do, given their abilities and circumstances, without comparisons to others. Instead of comparing ourselves with others, we could more profitably ask how well are we doing with what we have been given, and how far have we progressed recently.

Furthermore, if we are going to make comparisons, we should do it on the basis of several criteria, not just one or two. Let me give an example of how one criterion comparing happens in the Church. Suppose the Relief Society president needs a sister to lecture on home beautification. Obviously the woman she is going to ask to give the lecture is a woman with an immaculate, well-decorated home. The next week, wanting to have a lecture on how scriptures can help in a person's life, the president will invite somebody to speak who is a very good scriptorian. The following week, wanting to discuss home storage, she will have somebody come who has enough supplies to last through the Millennium.

If the other sisters choose to look at these women in a negative, comparative basis, they eventually find their self-esteem dropping. Rather than seeing Relief Society lessons as a word of encouragement, as a basis for gaining new understanding, or as a source of ideas, some women interpret the lessons to mean that they should already have the well-developed strengths of all these women. They ignore the possibility that the genealogist might be doing poorly in home beautification, and the scriptorian might have no food storage. I know of sisters who have gone home after some Relief Society lessons and literally withdrawn into lethargy, only to go back the next week to feel even more inadequate!

I am not criticizing the Relief Society; I am trying to point out that we all listen differently to messages. We have this "critical parent" part inside of us that may constantly make negative comparisons and undercut us in subtly destructive ways if we have not learned to listen appropriately.

I recommend that you compare yourself with yourself only. If you feel you must compare yourself with someone else, do it on the basis of at least thirty-five criteria. You may not bake as well as Jane, but you will probably find out that in the long run, using the thirty-five criteria you come out okay.

We need to be careful also to distinguish between judging ourselves on a relative or absolute basis. A patient of mine came to me depressed, anxious, and anhedonic (having no ability to experience pleasure). She had a long-standing tendency to compare herself with other people. She had converted to Mormonism in her mid-twenties, and her husband had also joined the Church. She had come from an economically, spiritually, and culturally impoverished family.

After joining the Church, she had striven for perfection in many areas. She had taken singing and piano lessons, and she had pushed herself hard to learn the various homemaking skills emphasized by the Relief Society. I have known very few people who had grown as much as she had in such a short time. So why was she suffering from depression and a negative self-image? In several of our conversations it became obvious that she had targeted another sister in the ward as a role model. This would have been fine if she had taken the other woman as a role model to help encourage her to do better, but instead she had taken her on as a model of perfection, as something to compare herself against. This is a dangerous error.

One day she told me in despair how much more accomplished this lady was than she, how much better she was at piano playing, singing, and doing all sorts of homemaking things. After some counseling, she realized that she was comparing herself against somebody who had been given many more opportunities. However, if we could compare the amount of personal growth in the last twenty years, my patient had experienced far more growth than the other woman. This other woman, with whom she compared herself, had been raised in a strong, wealthy LDS family that gave her only the best in life. I think it is important to realize that God is only going to judge us according to what we become, taking into consideration those things that have been afforded us in our lives. He won't ask, "How come you're not like so and so?" but, "How well did you use the tools and the abilities you were given?" How will you answer?

Principle #3
The Difference Between Remorse and Guilt

Many scriptural references describe repentance as a way of putting things behind us and no longer focusing on our imperfections.

As a professional counselor and former bishop, I realize that many people refuse to allow themselves to be included in the scripture, "Man is that he might have joy." One reason for this is rooted in the belief that they may not be worthy of happiness and that happiness eventually causes sadness anyway. ("Things are going well for me—knock on wood!")

This kind of thinking has its roots in Northern European thinking, which has influenced American thought. It was shaped by early Christian doctrines, which saw God as merely tolerating man. Because of their belief that man had hopelessly fallen from God's grace because of original sin, people saw their lot in life, whether of poverty, sadness, sickness, or mental illness, as being predestined by God, as being the will of God because of their sinfulness. God was seen as the ultimate critical, damning parent. Going even farther back, this Judeo-Christian philosophy had roots in the ancient notion that you "should never let the Evil Eye know that things are going too well because it will then cause them to go bad." These traditions still have powerful influence over many descendants of those who had these beliefs. These people may try to preempt God's love, kindness, and acceptance because they feel they are not worthy of happiness. They worry that if they do attain happiness, things will soon go bad.

The Latter-day Saint faith teaches that opposition must exist in all things. This does not mean that bad is *caused* by good. Bad things do happen to good people, but there is not a causal relationship; they do not happen as a result of their goodness.

To understand how this belief persists and how we can deal with it, we need to understand the concept of preemption. Let me first explain preemption in a civil context. Let's say, for example, that some city has a referendum on the ballot for the segregation of bathrooms on the basis of race. That is, blacks and whites could not use the same bathrooms. Suppose that in this community, seventy percent of the people vote "yes" on this ordinance, but on appeal the Supreme Court decides the new law is unconstitutional. The people then say, "Wait a minute. We choose to do our own thing here in this community. We voted this in, and we therefore refuse to accept the Supreme Court's decision." Most people would agree the town was preempting the constitution; they are putting themselves before the supreme law of the land.

It is not at all uncommon for people to hold tenaciously onto guilt in the same way that these people held on to what they considered to be their rights. A woman once came to me who had participated in an adulterous relationship many years previously. Although she had confessed to other bishops, she told me, too, what an awful person she was and said she was confident that God could not love her. She continued on about how she still felt black in her heart. As I realized that she had changed her behaviors and rectified the situation as best she could, I advised her to get on with living and let the guilt go as it served no more useful purpose in her life. She replied that this was not true, that the ugliness (the internalized guilt and shame) was going to have to remain with her forever.

Well, suppose I sent her to a stake president and eventually even to the President of the Church, and they told her the same thing: "Forgive yourself and forget this problem." If she chose not to do that, she would be preempting, in a very real way, the government of the Church. She is basically saying, "I do not accept God's government in my life. Neither do I accept his love, forgiveness, and concern for me."

Guilt serves a useful purpose only when it encourages us to repent or to change some behavior that is incorrect, unlawful, or immoral. But once the repentance process has occurred, what purposes does persistent guilt really serve?

Some people tend to wallow in guilt. A mechanism seems to exist within them that will not allow them to feel good about themselves—to allow the guilt to leave and to get on living a full and happy life. Yet once a person has repented and given up the incorrect behavior, continued guilt becomes counter-productive and corrodes a person's self-image.

Many people continue to do wrong because their low self-image makes them feel unworthy of God's love. They may have eschewed the behavior and repented to proper priesthood authority, but if they hold onto the guilt, they may choose to go back to the old behavior. The message they hear is "I've repented and given up my old ways, and I am still guilty and unhappy. So what good was repentance?" The natural reaction is to see this as justification to revert back to old behaviors.

Through this self-defeating pattern, they undermine themselves and continue to feed their grieving process. Certainly our critical parent ego state is more than happy to remind us of our past transgressions. It continually brings up the past, punishes us with it, and refuses to allow us to move on. The continual feelings of guilt eventually bog us down and create different types of depression.

These guilty feelings may become internalized growing beyond guilt and remorse. The person adopts a deep-seated negativism and poor self-image. Instead of hearing that what they did was stupid, dumb, mistaken, sinful, or even bad, they hear "I am a stupid, dumb, mistaken, sinful, and bad person." The negativism, worthlessness, and hopelessness become part of the personality and identity rather than just a feeling. It therefore becomes difficult to change and to let go of the negative patterns and guilt.

There are many things we may appropriately feel badly about. But we are innocent of many things that others (especially Satan and his cohorts) would have us feel guilty about. If we have repented of our wrong, we should then shun guilt that does not belong to us.

Perhaps the greatest example of forgiveness being offered, forgiveness being accepted, and guilt being cast off is in the New Testament when the adulteress was brought to Christ. Her accusers asked Christ what they should do with the woman. The Savior thoughtfully knelt down and doodled in the sand. Then he stood and said, "He that is without sin among you, let him first cast a stone at her." Everyone sheepishly dropped their stones and drifted away. After they had left, the Master looked upon the woman and asked, "Woman, where are those thine accusers? Hath no man condemned thee?"

She said, "No man, Lord."

And Jesus said unto her, "Neither do I condemn thee: go, and sin no more." (John 8:7–11.)

Could you imagine the Savior saying, "Go thy way and sin no more, but first burn a big red 'S' on your forehead, wear sackcloth, and throw ashes in your hair for the rest of your life so everybody will know how bad you've been?" No. We are told to forgive ourselves and forget our sins, to no longer ruminate, brood, or dwell upon that wrong we have done.

Guilt can also be used as a tool for the manipulation of ourselves and others. I was once ordered by the court to go over to the county jail and evaluate a child molester who had been convicted repeatedly. When I introduced myself as the court appointed evaluator, he immediately burst into tears. He told me what a terrible person he was to have done this to children. He said that he was not worth saving. His show of guilt was quite impressive, but the message he was really trying to send me was quite devious. At the same time he was telling me to look at how awful he was, he was implying that he was really a good person because otherwise he wouldn't feel so awful. I can imagine him doing similar things to the judge, who occupies a parental role. And if the judge only listens to the guilt and tears, he may hear, "Please have mercy upon me because I am a good person, look how awful and terrible I feel," instead of "I am responsible for this."

If you have children, you can perhaps appreciate what I am saying here. If a child about to be punished can demonstrate enough remorse, we sometimes back off. However, if the child digs in, shows no remorse, or even projects the guilt back toward us, we tend to come down on him even harder. Many people have learned to project their own guilt in order to gain sympathy, empathy, and mercy. This not only happens in families and societies, it happens inside our own heads as well. The critical parent inside our heads unleashes a torrent of abuse unless we confess to how awful we feel and shed enough tears to get the parent to back off. But, oh, what a price we pay in loss of self-esteem and even depression for not standing up to the responsibility of getting the problem resolved.

The problem of guilt lingering after the sin's departure is an old and pervasive one. Nephi gave one of the best descriptions of the anguish we face and the insight that is our salvation:

> . . . My soul delighteth in the things of the Lord; and my heart pondereth continually upon the things which I have seen and heard.
>
> Nevertheless, notwithstanding the great goodness of the Lord, in showing me his great and marvelous works, my heart exclaimeth: *O wretched man that I am*! Yea, my heart sorroweth because of my flesh; my soul grieveth because of mine iniquities.
>
> I am encompassed about, because of the temptations and the sins which do so easily beset me.
>
> And when I desire to rejoice, my heart groaneth because of my sins; nevertheless, I know in whom I have trusted.
>
> My God hath been my support; he hath led me through mine afflictions in the wilderness . . .
>
> He hath filled me with his love. . . .
>
> Behold, he hath heard my cry by day, and he hath given me

> knowledge by visions in the night time . . .
>
> O then, if I have seen so great things, if the Lord in his condescension unto the children of men hath visited men in so much mercy, why should my heart weep and my soul linger in the valley of sorrow, and my flesh waste away, and my strength slacken, because of mine afflictions?
>
> And why should I yield to sin, because of my flesh? Yea, why should I give way to temptations, that the evil one have place in my heart to destroy my peace and afflict my soul? Why am I angry because of mine enemy?
>
> *Awake, my soul! No longer droop in sin.* Rejoice, O my heart, and give place no more for the enemy of my soul. (2 Nephi 4:16–21, 23, 26–28, emphasis added.)

We need to take Nephi's words to heart. Let guilt serve the purpose for which it was meant: to get us to change our behaviors. Once that change has occurred and we have done what we can, it is no longer necessary to "droop in sin" or to wallow in guilt. God doesn't love us only when we are righteous. He loves us always.

Principle #4
Avoid Absolutes and Death Equivalencies

I often hear patients say, "I can't stand this," "I'll die if I don't get . . . ," "I won't make it without. . . ." Such statements are what I call "death equivalencies." That is, the words and phrases imply a death-like circumstance to the mind. These words create tension, pressure, desperateness, and a type of hysteria, not only within the person saying them, but also in those around them. Whatever situation you face, try to describe it accurately. Make sure you use adjectives and descriptions that are proportionate to the events at hand.

Sometimes, it is important to help people redefine their problems in less drastic terms. Not surprisingly, a person who intervenes in a crisis uses words that are less traumatic or less dramatic than those used by the person who is in the so-called "crisis."

One woman told me that her husband was a clerk in their ward and that they had to travel several miles to church. After the meetings her husband had to stay after church for thirty to forty-five minutes every Sunday. During this time, the woman had to wait. She said to me, "It is awful waiting; I can't stand it. In fact, it's tormenting."

Tormenting? I associate that with the word "torture." Torture is where they pour acid down your nose, crush your knuckles, or put bamboo slivers under your fingernails. Waiting is not tormenting. I can accept that it is boring, even uncomfortable for her, but not tormenting. She could, of course, completely redefine the situation and see it in a positive light—as an opportunity to visit, for example. But even if she does choose to view the waiting in a negative sense, she should not overdramatize the situation by using such an exaggerated term.

If we are in a situation that we feel is life-threatening, our adrenaline system activates the body's "fight or flight" mechanism. This is a very useful thing if we have to defend ourselves or run for our lives. But a vocabulary built on death equivalencies makes less drastic problems seem much more severe. Whenever I hear people say something is "terrible," "horrible," "catastrophic," or "tormenting," or they say, "I can't stand it," or "I'm not going to make it," I fear for them. Very few events in life truly warrant those extreme adjectives. What do these people do when a *real* catastrophe occurs? How do they manage the death of an immediate family member or some other real tragedy?

One of the major differences between man and beast is man's ability to use symbols and language. Our language is like a program telling our computer-brain how to interpret the situation. If we tell our computer that something is horrible, it believes us and sends instructions to act appropriately. Thus, we will overreact and cause ourselves unnecessary pain and trauma. If on a scale of one to ten (one being the worst and ten being the best), we only think in ones and tens, our minds begin to fail us because the mind cannot handle ones and tens very long. If we really are in a one or ten situation, it is helpful to remember these situations usually have two qualities: they are temporary and isolated. If you are in the rut of using words in the one or ten category, here is a list suggesting words for each number on that scale that may help you find the more stable middle ground.

1. Terrible, awful, devastating, catastrophic, tormenting, worst-that-could-happen, hell
2. Humiliating, painful, uncomfortable, unnerving, troublesome, upsetting, annoying, embarrassing, aggravating, stressful, back-sliding, deflating, intense, stressful
3. Boring, wearying, inconvenient, untimely
4. Ordinary, habitual, mediocre, routine, mundane, practical
5. Average, usual, everyday, common

6. Above average, good, okay, encouraging, adequate
7. Fun, exciting, enjoyable, surprising
8. Thrilling, exhilarating, stimulating, refreshing, cheerful
9. Great, delightful, awesome, super, sensational, terrific, amazing, astounding
10. Wonderful, glorious, fantastic, heavenly, once-in-a-lifetime, marvelous

Not surprisingly, if we say things that make our situation more "glorious" or "fantastic" than it really is, our computer-brain will likewise be fooled. We may lose our composure and become less effective. Young people are often prone to exaggerated thinking. Suzy meets Johnny. He is wonderful, glorious, celestial—truly a godsend. Consequently, she can't do her math or her English because her mind is focused on this fantastic and heavenly thing that has happened to her. Then one day Suzy finds Johnny holding hands with Jane. This is a catastrophe. She can't stand it. And of course, she's immobilized again: she can't do her math, she can't do her English, and she becomes withdrawn and isolated. If this continues, it can be a truly dangerous situation. She is making mountains out of molehills—a practice that is severely affecting her life. If this goes on too long, she may fail school. The results of making mountains out of molehills is similar for adults.

"Can't" is also a death equivalency because the only reason we cannot do a thing is because we are dead! When people say they cannot face this or that, their brain believes them and the people simply give up trying. If people say, "I find it uncomfortable dealing with myself" or "To take that class would upset me," then I can buy that. But "can't" usually leads to paralysis. One way that people avoid looking at themselves or making needed changes in their lives is to say, "I can't come in and talk" or "I can't stand to listen to those things."

Another death equivalency that causes a great amount of havoc in people's lives is the attitude that they *have* to have something. To "have to have" something rather than just "wanting" it implies an emergent crisis, and it is this kind of thinking that can catapult us into negative circumstances. Also, there is a major difference between wanting something and seeing it as an absolute necessity essential for your survival.

Some common notions that fall into this category are as follows:

1) I *must* have everyone's approval, love, and respect.
2) I *must* have guarantees. If I am going to try something, I

must know that it will be successful.

3) I *must* have my own way.
4) Other people *must* think, feel, and act the way I think they should.

Wanting these things is not dangerous; in fact, wanting them is normal. The danger comes when we think having these things is an *absolute necessity*. The next four principles are based on overcoming these dangerous attitudes.

Principle #5
Don't Expect Approval

No matter what we do, we cannot get everybody to like us and yet trying to please everyone is a common problem. People who do this become emotional chameleons and intellectual prostitutes. In one group they appear to adhere to one value system and to represent a certain set of feelings and thoughts. In another group, however, they reflect totally different values, thoughts, and feelings. They placate others and discount their own values and ideas in a desperate attempt to get all people to like them.

But if we spend our whole lives trying to become what others want us to become or trying to do what others want us to do and never really standing up for what we think, we eventually realize that we have no stable values and we are catapulted into depression.

Principle #6
Life Gives No Guarantees

Like attempting to be perfect all at once, the demand for guarantees is also paralyzing. Our society has become so success oriented that many people have become fearful of trying anything without the guarantee that they will succeed. While we may *want* guarantees, if we feel we *must* have them, we will stop most activities in our lives and become paralyzed with fear.

In this life we have to take risks in thoughts and action in spite of possible failure. We have to remember that failure can actually be a success, if from it we learn new and better ways of thinking and doing. Certainly, no athlete ever became great without failing many times. Life would be a lot easier if we had guarantees, but guarantees are rarely found in life. If you buy a new car, take the guarantee. But for the other areas in your life, realize that caution and good judgment are probably all you will have working for you.

Principle #7
Don't Expect the World to Revolve Around You

Some people are so self-centered that they cannot stand to hear the word "no." If they are thwarted in their activities, they throw a temper tantrum or sulk. Mature people recognize the need for compromise in most day-to-day matters and strive to understand that their values must allow for flexibility. Compromise is the way mature people deal with each other in our society.

But neurotic thinkers don't allow for compromise. Not only do they want to impose their will upon others, they often want to impose their mythologies about life on others as well. Remember the scripture: "When I was a child, I spake as a child, I understood as a child, I thought as a child: but when I became a man, I put away childish things." (1 Cor. 13:11.) Well, many people have not yet put away their childish things. It is important to realize that we were programmed as children. When this programming occurred, we were naive. We lacked the experience needed to be able to reject or accept what was offered. Now that we are adults we must "put away childish things" and choose the beliefs and thoughts that we can logically accept and maintain as adults.

Principal #8
Give Others Freedom of Thought and Action

As we discussed in the chapter on free agency, we fought and won a great war in heaven for the right to choose. We will not like some of the choices people make, but we must let them choose anyway. We have the responsibility to encourage, admonish, and teach correct principles, but others have the freedom and the obligation to choose for themselves.

> No power or influence can or ought to be maintained by virtue of the priesthood, only by persuasion, by long-suffering, by gentleness and meekness, and by love unfeigned;
>
> By kindness, and pure knowledge, which shall greatly enlarge the soul without hypocrisy, and without guile. (D&C 121:41–42)

Principle #9
Learn to Control Anger

Anger is one of the most destructive forces known to man. The amount of energy needed to sustain anger is amazing. In the Sermon on the Mount, Christ made clear that "whosoever is angry with his brother without cause shall be in danger of the judgment." (Matt.

5:22.) This warning becomes even stronger when he says, "Love your enemies, bless them that curse you, do good to them that hate you, and pray for them which despitefully use you, and persecute you." (Matt. 5:44.) These admonitions should give us additional reasons to learn how to handle the basic emotion of anger.

As a "natural man," I would be less than honest if I didn't admit that when somebody hurts me, my natural inclination is to hurt them back. I find I am not alone in this.

One time I heard a story that impressed me deeply. It seems two haberdashers had stores across the street from one another and had, over the years, become bitter competitors. They would spend a great deal of time standing in the doorway scrutinizing one another's business. When one would get a customer, he would smile in triumph at the other one and take the new client inside. Their rivalry and anger grew unchecked for many years. One night an angel appeared to one of the men in a dream. The angel said, "God has sent me here to teach you a very great lesson. God will grant you whatever you wish, but you must understand that whatever you are granted, your competitor across the street will be given twice as much. Would you be rich? You may be richer than a king, but he will be still richer. Would you have children that you may be proud of and that are famous? You may, but he will have more children and they will be more famous. Would you live a long and healthy life? You may, but his life will be longer and healthier." The man frowned and pondered for a considerable time. Finally he told the angel, "I wish to be struck blind in one eye."

Anger must be controlled or it will destroy us. While there is only one healthy method, there seem to be five basic ways people handle anger. Often people use a mixture of the five.

1) *Passivity*. Many people have a way of just swallowing anger; in the classic jargon, they "repress" it. Such people commonly have somatic or physical problems. The anger often manifests itself in gastrointestinal distress, headaches, hypertension, or heart palpitations. Evidence shows that these symptoms compound many other disorders and can even reduce our resistance to things such as the common cold, flu, or cancer.

2) *Explosiveness or aggressiveness*. People often demonstrate their anger through a bombardment of physical or verbal activities. At the extremes, they end up destroying relationships or marriages, frequently losing jobs, or having altercations with the law.

3) *The pressure cooker model.* In this model, people remain passive and bite the bullet until they just cannot stand it any more. Finally, their anger results in aggressive physical and/or verbal manifestations. I call this management system the "seagull fashion." It is like the father who isolates himself from his family by watching T.V. or doing his own little projects until something in the family irritates him sufficiently, then he swoops down on the family, squawking loudly and attacking everyone only to end up isolating himself again. The problem in this example is lack of consistency. While the father may have a very good lesson he is trying to teach, those being attacked remember only the father's unpredictable behavior. Violence is a poor teacher.

4) *Passive-aggressiveness.* Like the old haberdashers, some people literally hurt *themselves* as a way of getting even with other people. Passive–aggressive people often feel powerless. Their passive behavior is a way of getting even without using open, hostile ways. Children, for example, may use procrastination, stubborness, dawdling, or forgetfulness as weapons.

An employee who is angry with his boss may use these same methods to get back at the boss. He does things the boss cannot respond to and thus the employee remains safe. Such behaviors create anger and frustration in all those involved and may slowly break down good family and work environments.

5) *Assertiveness.* This pattern of response has proven so successful that shelves full of "How to Respond Assertively" books have been written. Some of them are quite effective in teaching people to take timely, measured responses to the sources of agitation in their lives.

Simply put, assertiveness requires consistent honesty. When assertive people are angry, they show their anger in a consistent way. Communication and problem solving guidelines explained elsewhere in this book apply here and could help us learn to deal with anger constructively. Be assured, though, that hitting, name-calling, and attacking are not part of assertiveness or good teaching (see Chapter 9).

One of my patients complained bitterly about people at work who were constantly telling racial, ethnic, or religious jokes. He was very sensitive to these issues and was quite anxious about the situation. However, instead of responding consistently to their slurs, explaining that he thought their jokes were inappropriate, he had been responding in the pressure cooker mode, reacting passively until he could stand it no longer and then exploding and causing a scene. I pointed out that his inconsistency was actually showing some acceptance of their behavior and that in order to change anything he would have to be *consistent* in walking away or in stating his feelings. I learned later that after consistently using comments like "Excuse me, but I don't listen to ethnic jokes" and "I have problems with racial or religious stories. Please don't tell them around me," things changed in a positive way. His anxiety was relieved.

One of the most important options for dealing with anger is to simply remove yourself from the anger-creating situation altogether. When discussions and contracts have failed, a temporary escape may be the answer. I remember placing one woman under hospitalization who was obviously overwhelmed with anger and confusion. She wept often and violently. Between her tears were accusations about issues: "If my husband wouldn't do this . . . " "If only my children would do this. . . ." She told me I was placing the wrong person in the hospital and that she was merely a victim. I agreed with her in many respects, but I told her it is not unusual for victims to go to the hospital because, as in this case, it isn't practical to hospitalize ten other people instead. In the hospital she got into a safe environment where she could "unplug" for awhile and sort out her feelings. Eventually, counseling improved her family situation.

Principle #10
Accept Trials as Learning Experiences

I recently read something that summarizes my feelings about this principle:

The Barren Branches of December

If a smile may linger upon lips once laughing, so shall a tear ever swell within the eye once weeping. For the mind turns not easily aside and memories fade not quickly for those who accept the bitter with the sweet, the last with the first. For who remembers the bloom upon the tree or the blush of the fruit in its fullness without also the barren branches of December? Likewise, the dawn is nothing without the night which preceeds it, nor can the star show forth its brilliance without the darkness surrounding.

And such, it seems, is the order of all things. Unto all is given opposition, yet December shall pass, the darkness flee, and nothing continues unending. For which of us sees the sun rise, yet never fall; the flame burn, yet not consume; the bud blossom, yet never fade; and which of the seasons begin and have no end?

Have we part in the order of all things? Do we not struggle in our search for happiness? Know we love without also loneliness, success without failure, or joy without first pain? Do we not suffer illness? Do we not grow weary?

Yet, shall we fully condemn our difficulties? The lump of clay is worked, formed and fiercely fired—but does it not emerge a thing of strength and beauty? The autumn flower dies a bitter death in winter's freezing grip, but in dying drops its seed, ensuring its own continuance. Is not the flower victorious? And now I ask, does the clay condemn the refiner's fire, or the seed the winter freeze? Unto us it is given to know that trials do not last forever, for the earth moves across the heavens, and time stands not idle. Neither does the earth remain unchanged, nor anything which is upon it. Does a seed within the soil remain a seed forever? Does a small stream continue a stream forever? No, it flows on its way to a river; nor does the river spring from humble beginnings. And like the stream, we grow and increase, until at last we, too, shall meet, like the river and the sea, with each past sorrow simply a grain of sand over which we dwell.

And so we see that unto every beginning is given an end, and unto the sorrowful moment is appointed the hour of joy—as surely as the storm is followed by the sun, and the heat of day soothed by the cool of night. Would we sacrifice the sun to be rid of the storm, never savor the cool to be spared the heat? No, for a world with one and not the other is a world untried, a world unfulfilled. It is the heavens with the sun, but without the moon or stars. It is a song once written, but never sung. And what is the sweet without the bitter, or the first without the last? For who remembers the bloom upon the tree or the blush of the fruit in its fullness, without also the barren branches of December?

By Janice A. Richardson
(Used by Permission)

As we grow and develop, we realize that we are in a honing process—we are being polished. I am confident that God allows friction and abrasion to happen to us in order to polish off our rough edges. Another word for "friction" is "trials." Sometimes these trials can grow to true crisis proportions, but our attitudes about these trials can make them either growing experiences or experiences that stop our progress. In many languages, the word crisis implies both danger and opportunity. A crisis, by its very nature, is not a neutral event. It will always affect us in some way. We can make the choice of how a crisis will affect us and what we will do with the crisis. How we use the energy from a crisis determines the ultimate result of the crisis. The outcome is up to us.

A crisis can be a very creative time when we have the right attitudes. I believe that from the worst crises, many great things can happen. For example, suppose a small community is the site of a terrible murder. This tragedy could turn into a disaster if the citizens form lynch mobs or isolate themselves in barricaded homes. If, on the other hand, the town responds by installing new lighting systems, looking at law enforcement needs, and upgrading its community support systems, the crises could become creative and functional.

It took a great crisis in my own life to teach me that a devastating experience can also be a learning experience. My parents died when I was a young man. My brother and sister lived with relatives while I remained with foster parents. In my late teens, I became interested in the gospel of Jesus Christ and subsequently went on a mission, a major turning point in my life. After I returned from my mission and married, my wife and I took over the legal guardianship of my fifteen-year-old brother, who was having some difficulties as a teenager. My brother and I grew very close.

When he was seventeen, we moved to Wyoming where I was to do my graduate work. After living there for five weeks, my brother went to a youth dance. On the dance floor, four young men beat my brother to death. They didn't mean to kill him, but that didn't make any difference—he was dead just the same. I was called at one-thirty in the morning by an abrupt, angry-sounding police officer who asked if I was Zane Nelson and if I had a brother by the name of Scott Nelson. I told him I did. He said, "I'm at the Laramie Memorial Hospital with your brother. He dropped dead on a dance floor."

After identifying the body, I came back from the hospital numb, overwhelmed with confusion and pain. For several days I experienced a psychic numbing and somehow managed to get through the funeral and burial. But for many nights afterward, crazed with pain and confusion, I screamed out my anger toward God and toward my parents. I felt they had all abandoned me with an unbearable burden.

I was obsessed with hurt and pain. I withdrew socially and wallowed in self-pity and blame. I finally realized, through the help of one of my professors, that I was giving up psychologically and that I had to turn my behaviors around.

After a good deal of prayer, my wife and I decided that the only way I was going to get rid of this depression was to become involved in other things. We made a commitment at that time to do missionary work and to complete the graduate program I had started. This rededication to positive goals pulled me away from my singular focus on my pain. I quit brooding, ruminating, and being angry over my brother's death (a futile state that had only led me to deeper and deeper despair). As a consequence of real commitment to these creative goals, we enjoyed some fun and fruitful missionary efforts and a good graduate school experience.

Major crises can obscure all other problems in the lives of the people affected. But I cannot stress enough that crises will cripple us only when we *let* them overshadow all other aspects of our lives. People can make any negative situation so monstrous in their minds that they convince themselves of the impossibility of coping. This fear then is manifested as anger or desperation, often ending with tragic consequences.

One such situation sticks in my mind. My specialty is suicidology, and I am often called in by coroners on unusual cases. Some time ago I was called to a home where an eleven-year-old boy had apparently taken his own life with a high-powered rifle. There was no note, and the boy had seemed to be a happy member of an integrated family. What had caused this seemingly intelligent and well-adjusted youngster to turn the rifle on himself? It turned out that he had stayed home from school and become bored. Looking for something to do he began playing with his dad's shotgun and rifle. The shotgun accidentally discharged, blowing a hole in a piece of antique furniture. In the overly intense aftermath that always follows an accident like that, the boy's fear of what he had done led him to kill himself.

On the other hand, crises can provide the opportunity for positive change if we make the right choices. I recall a friend of mine who had gone blind from the effects of diabetes. He and his wife came to visit me during the time he was in rehabilitative training. When they got up to leave, I instinctively reached out to help him find his cane. His wife shook her head and I watched as he walked right into a desk. His wife said casually, "You need to be more careful where you are going, dear." She was overcoming the natural inclination to help him too much, thus helping him to become independent. He went on to become a significant force in the education of the blind in Idaho. His wife could have chosen to make him dependent on her, and this man could have stayed at home and felt sorry for himself. Both their choices in the face of a major crisis helped him become a happy, productive person.

A crisis situation is certainly not the only time when we can grow or change. We will have ample non-crisis tests, both in this life and the next. My concern is not only that we make it through the crises and tests, but that we make it through with the self-esteem, humility, faith, determination, toughness, and compassion that we need to discover the joy that should be inherent in our journey.

SANITY STRATEGY #9

People Are FRAGILE: Handle With Care

In *The Writings of Lazarus Long,* Robert A. Heinlein said,

> Moving parts in rubbing contact require lubrication to avoid excessive wear. Honorifics and formal politeness provide lubrication where people rub together. Often the very young, the untravelled, the naive, the unsophisticated deplore these formalities as "empty, meaningless, or dishonest" and scorn the use of them. No matter how pure their motives, they thereby throw sand into the machinery which does not work too well at best.

Relationships require lubrication but too often get sand. People often come into my office and express their desire to help and change some key person in their life, feeling that "if only" that person would change, they would both be happier and their problems would be solved. However, the only way to influence others to positive change is to initiate positive change in ourselves. Only as we learn new problem-solving and communication skills, for example, and therefore deal with these key people in our lives in a more lubricating and less sand-throwing way, can we can be a powerful catalyst for change in their lives.

Communicating Feelings

Many problems could be resolved if we could effectively communicate and deal with problems appropriately. Effective communication is difficult, but it is an essential tool in discovering, nurturing, or changing feelings. People see the world in different ways. One person's lubrication is another person's hypocrisy. We don't have to accept each others views in order to communicate, but we do have to respect them.

Many times communication, bad or good, is based on someone trying to communicate feelings. They want to express their emotions and perhaps they want to have a catharsis. They basically do not want a response but just someone to listen to them. Another time, they may really want help in solving a problem. It is interesting to note that men often have a hard time just *listening* to feelings. Rather, they come into my office with the idea that when they hear feelings, they are supposed to *do* something. Since it is often impossible for them to do anything about their wives' feelings, they become frustrated and compound the difficulty of the situation. Wives do their husbands a service when they help them understand that some of the time all they need is someone to listen.

Communication Guidelines

As I present some guidelines for communication and problem solving, keep in mind that I'm not saying they all have to be followed in normal, routine conversation, although it would be beneficial. I can say, without equivocation, that when I am wise enough to follow them, my ability to understand others and to help them solve their differences and problems increases dramatically. If we choose not to follow these guidelines, we may find ourselves sabotaging some of the great talents and blessings that God has given us.

1. *Use "I" messages while avoiding "you" messages.*

When people hear the word "you," they often sense that they are under siege. When we avoid "you" messages, however, we help pull down defenses. For example, I was counseling a woman who was a whiner. As she told me her story, she would whine like a fire engine. You can imagine that if it bothered me, her therapist, then it drove her husband up the wall. The "natural man" in me was aching to say, "Good grief, lady! Where did YOU learn to talk? When YOU raise and lower YOUR voice like that, YOU'RE a complete turnoff!"

Had I approached her with that kind of message, I would not have been able to help the couple. Instead, I said to her, "As a psychologist, I need to think clearly; however, I have noticed that sometimes my mind wanders and I don't stay focused on what people are saying. When somebody raises and lowers their voice with me, old episodes of my life keep intruding on my thoughts."

The woman understood and for the next twenty minutes did very well. Then she started into her whine again. As soon as she did that, I said, "Excuse me, but I noticed that I was becoming distracted again." It solved our problem.

2. *Avoid blaming others.*

Similar to the "you" messages, when we start to blame the other person for everything that is wrong and refuse to shoulder some of the responsibility ourselves, we only make matters worse. The real danger in trying to tend everybody else's doorstep is that we remain oblivious to our own behaviors and attitudes, which may be part of the problem.

3. *Feedback, Repeat back, Paraphrase.*

In some situations, it is important to repeat or to paraphrase what has just been said. "Are you saying that . . ." or "In other words, what you mean is. . . ." This is a straightforward way of reassuring people that they are being listened to and understood.

4. *Avoid all-inclusive words: never, always, every time. . . .*

These assertions are usually wrong and, therefore, distracting. For example, if the wife says, "You never take me out," the husband usually does not hear the message she is trying to convey, which is: "I would like to go out with you more often." Instead, he hears only the word "never," and comes back with something like, "Six weeks ago I took you to McDonald's, and now I *never* take you out?" It should be clear that both conversation partners get trapped by these all-inclusive words.

5. *Use "parent" communications sparingly. These usually include key words such as should, have to, ought to, must, mustn't.*

If we could only listen as well as we can hear, how much farther along we would be! Most people do not like to be parented, and *should*, *have to*, *ought to*, *must*, and *mustn't* are among the most effective words for killing a conversation.

6. *Never tell someone how they think or feel.*

This is an enormous turn off. People will often take issue with your interpretation of their feelings and become more irritable and angry. The predictable result is that they simply stop listening.

7. *Don't argue facts but try to understand feelings.*

As I have pointed out earlier, facts are not as important as the feelings involved. To argue over whether someone was one hour late or forty-five minutes late or whether someone was gone every night of the week or only four nights is absurd. The feelings those facts incurred are what really count. Express the feelings you are having and see how much more productive the conversation will become.

8. *Do not use physical or verbal threats or abuse.*

Screams and threats are powerful messages in their own right—so powerful, in fact, that they focus attention *away* from the intended message. The fist as a reinforcer smashes the framework of trust and understanding. The scream drowns out the words.

9. *Avoid placating.*

Don't just tell people what they want to hear and don't coerce people into agreeing with you. Encouraging intellectual and emotional prostitution in others is not a good teaching method, nor does it promote openness and honesty in the relationship.

10. *Avoid sarcasm.*

Ideally, humor should demonstrate new ways of solving problems. Humor can also help us put our problems in perspective without distracting our energy for solving them. Sarcasm, however, is the easiest and cheapest form of humor and does not accomplish anything.

Humor provides an oil or lubrication in life. When we lose our ability to see the funny side of life it becomes burdensome and dull! The right kind of humor and laughter lightens everyone's load. Sarcasm, on the other hand, is humor at someone's expense and is rarely funny to anyone but often causes ill will.

11. *Deal with one issue at a time.*

The danger here is twofold. By bringing up too many issues at once, the conversation can become so overwhelming that one or both parties will become defensive and sabotage the discussion. Also, the presence of many issues might water down the conversation to the point where no issues are really confronted and feelings about the futility of discussion are reinforced.

12. *Be aware of non-verbal responses.*

The set jaw, the clenched or shaking fist, the facial grimaces—all of these convey messages to us. The blow is the non-verbal counterpart of the scream. If it ever comes to this, you can usually be sure you have already missed many subtle messages that led up to it.

13. *Avoid interrupting.*

To interrupt somebody is the same as telling them we are not listening. When you feel like interrupting, try to channel the urge by paraphrasing what the person has said. It is more polite and more productive.

14. *Avoid lecturing.*

People have a way of becoming "deaf" when something is directed at them for too long. Leave the speech-making for professors and politicians.

15. *Avoid hidden agendas.*

Communication should be honest and open. Hidden agendas should be avoided. When people are deliberately trying to guide the conversation into what they want it to be or to get what they would like in a situation, it becomes dishonest. This communication pattern creates suspiciousness and guardedness in people.

16. *Take a time-out.*

People often sense that they've reached a point in a discussion when they're about to say something they'll regret. If your adrenaline is running high, and your computer is getting hot, you should withdraw from the conversation and come back to it later.

Sometimes people will not allow the other person to break out of a conversation. They insist that they are going to talk about it "right now." But it's very important to realize that we have to wait for our communication opportunities. The key to withdrawing gracefully is the assurance that you are willing to revisit the issue when tempers have cooled.

17. *Don't say "I told you so!"*

Nobody likes to hear evidence that they are wrong or stupid.

18. *Make an appointment to talk about problems.*

It makes sense to set aside time for discussing problems because it helps avoid talking about them *all* the time.

Sometimes marriages become so problem oriented that husband and wife do not take time to enjoy themselves or those qualities in their partner that made marriage to him or her desirable—problems begin to dominate the conversations. The only topics of discussion become the washing machine, the bald tires on the car, the holes in the roof, the budget, and Johnny's bed-wetting. These discussions can become very painful and overwhelming. And while they cannot be ignored, the relationship cannot thrive if problems are always at the forefront of the discussion.

What I recommend is to have an allotted time every week when issues can be identified and discussed one by one and the best working solution adopted. Then, the problems should be left until the next scheduled time for discussion.

Finally, remember, if one person has a communication problem, you both have—and it is against the rules to tell the other person they are breaking these rules.

Contracting

Another effective element of an overall strategy for interpersonal problem solving is called contracting. In a negative light, a contract can be an adversarial document between two people who don't trust one another. When used in a positive manner, when those involved have a good attitude or spirit and have no desire to manipulate or nitpick, a contract is a very useful document to help clarify roles and expectations in non-adversarial situations. When used properly contracts provide consistency and predictability in human relations.

Contracting in family situations can reduce much of the friction that usually comes with close interpersonal relationships. Again though, a contract is only as good as the *spirit* or the *attitude* of those involved. If someone decides to be secretive, devious, nagging, or rigid, the contract will not work. Indeed, under those conditions, it can become a tool for abuse. But, when approached with a good spirit and a good attitude, when all those involved desire success and happiness, contracts can clarify and help smooth out some of the ruffles often experienced in personal relationships.

Typically, effective contracts distinguish between three major elements: rights, privileges, and rules.

Rights are something we have by virtue of being human beings in a free society. They don't have to be earned or justified. In most nations, rights are guaranteed by a constitution and cannot be infringed upon by the family.

Privileges are bestowed upon people by virtue of their standing, good behavior, or accomplishments. If a person does not show discretion, his privileges can be withdrawn. As far as the state is concerned, a driver's license is a privilege, not a right. In a family, privileges include things like access to a car and entertainment opportunities.

A rule is a boundary. For your state, twenty-five miles per hour may be as fast as you can go in the city. For a family, rules typically include curfew times, duration and frequency of telephone calls, work or chore expectations, or the manner of settling disputes between family members.

A few suggestions should be made on contracting:

1) The contract should not establish expectations for only one person. If the document is to work, it should fit all parties. While some privileges are afforded by age and status, parents should avoid establishing conditions which they are not willing to commit to or live by themselves. Parents invite problems when they expect more from a child than they do from themselves.

2) When enforcing contracts, remember: live by the spirit and do not get caught up in the letter of the law. For example, if a contract limits personal phone calls to thirty minutes, it should be only a general guideline and not something where a stopwatch is used.

3) The contract should be written in a way that applies to all family members and does not make any one person feel that he or she is the focus. Wordings should be used to imply "we" or "the family," rather than a specific person.

4) The rewards and consequences should be spelled out. People want structure and want to know what to expect. Feelings need to be clarified and dealt with to a point where the people *want* to make the contract work. Then enforcement of the contract should be done with love so that the spirit of the contract is not broken.

Because it's important not to overburden the "spirit" of the contract, contracts should be as specific as possible. The more specific the contracts are, the easier they will be to follow. The less often one party of the contract can say, "That wasn't clear," the fewer disputes there will be. Contracts clarify roles and positions so people can predict major confrontations and, to a certain extent, avoid wars that only result in petty victories. Contracting is not exclusively an interpersonal tool. Contracting with yourself can be productive too. Every New Year's Day, people commit to stop smoking, stop swearing, or stop acting in some other particular way. Most of those who successfully keep those commitments are those who use a program based on some value clarification exercise.

Contracting is only one tool available to those searching for solutions to interpersonal frictions and looking for ways to help those they love; however, it is a tool that has two advantages: it offers an excellent opportunity to clarify concerns, and it seeks some balance of reward and responsibility among the parties involved.

Effectively Teaching Correct Principles

We have been instructed to teach correct principles and let people govern themselves. We fought for this right to govern ourselves in the war in heaven and are now exercising that right here on earth. But as we watch those in the process of ruining their lives and the lives of others through the use of their free agency, it is easy to question the wisdom of free agency. I don't think there is anything more frustrating than to watch somebody freely choosing his way to destruction while you must refrain from intervening directly. At times intervention may be appropriate (as with certain cases of drug and alcohol addiction), since people may be out of control and unable to help themselves. Nevertheless, this is the exception, and our primary job with others remains to teach correct principles and let them govern themselves.

So how do we go about teaching correct principles? Sometimes we teach correct principles very badly, using immature or even brutal tactics. When parents suddenly blow up in a barrage of physical and/or verbal abuse directed at a child, the parents appear erratic and inconsistent. Instead of teaching correct principles, such behaviors only teach fear, anger, and inconsistency.

After such an outburst most parents recognize that the problem occurred when they were in a child ego state or a critical parent ego state. But this awareness, by itself, usually doesn't help correct the problem. Only when people are open to understand the dynamics of teaching and learning can they interpret their feelings and correct their behavior. In those moments when anger and frustration threaten to turn the attempt to teach or enforce good principles into a family war, how can you negotiate peace? First, you must get your parent ego under control.

Whereas the parent is ideally a teacher, the parent ego is, by definition, a disciplinarian. The parent ego is quite principled, but sometimes has an overwhelming obsession with right and wrong. The parent ego is usually right in principle, but wrong in actions.

We can minimize the parent disciplinarian ego by assisting it as we did the regular critical parent ego. First we must resist the urge to kick parent disciplinarian ego out. Let me use an example: I have seen many mothers and fathers who are very grateful and happy to have a priesthood advisor or a bishop or mutual teacher say, "Let me assist you in bridging some of the communication problems between you and your daughter." On the other hand, I have also seen leaders in these same positions tell parents to leave the kid alone and to stop doing this or stop doing that, and try to take over. In response, the parents often become defensive and hostile.

We need to treat our parent disciplinarian ego as a good leader would treat parents. Instead of attacking parents he would make sure they know he wanted to assist them, but that he does not want to take the responsibility for their children or take the parents out of the picture. He would assure the parents that he absolutely believes their principles are correct and he is only there to assist them in teaching these principles. He would let the parents know he empathizes with them and the fears or frustrations they feel. If done sincerely, this takes away the threat to the parent-ego. If we can use this same process with our disciplinarian parent ego, we are more likely to develop communication patterns that will be encouraging, and not discouraging to our own children. Since we want to teach and the child naturally wants to learn, if they pull away from us we can be sure it is our tactics that are the problem. The most important thing a teacher or parent can do is to protect and encourage the child's curiosity, growth, and natural desire to learn.

Once my ten-year-old son, Brock, was a guest at one of my friends' homes. While my friend attempted to do some household chores, Brock dogged him with a series of questions like, "What is this? How does it work? Why do you need it?" Finally becoming tired of all the questions, my friend answered, "Just because. That's why." Brock stared him down and then said, "My dad says I can't learn from 'because' answers. That just means you don't want to answer the question." My friend, knowing that he was had, smiled.

A parent has the responsibility and the challenge to take the time and effort to teach, even when it is not convenient. When we seize the teaching moments we increase a child's desire to learn. As teachers of ourselves and others, we must be alert for those productive teaching opportunities—moments when the teacher is ready and the pupil is willing. Discovering teaching opportunities often takes a good deal of observation and alertness and a foundation of trust and confidence. When those key moments come, a good teacher is able to share his most challenging thoughts and comments in a positive or productive way.

Desire is one key to learning; insight is another. Just as we sometimes puzzle ourselves and others with our unexplained failures, we may mystify ourselves and others with our inexplicable successes. For most of us, insight comes by asking the right questions, although it is true that insight is probably not an absolute prerequisite for success. But while insight is certainly not needed to duplicate our shortcomings, it may well be a prerequisite for duplicating our successes.

A good teacher can help a willing student gain insight. Unfortunately, as every experienced teacher can attest, people (having left behind the eagerness and honesty of the small child) often avoid insight and understanding. Knowledge can be a burden as Alma noted when he asked, "How much more cursed [or encumbered] is he that knoweth the will of God and doeth it not, than he that only believeth, or only hath cause to believe?" (Alma 32:19.) We may truly believe that God wants to see each of us progress as individuals, but we may be frightened of finding out the difficulty of the next step in progression.

As we attempt to teach correct principles we need to remember that with knowledge comes both *freedom* and *responsibility*—a freedom from ignorance, but a responsibility to think and act in light of that knowledge. This is the reason mental health professionals ask not only, "Does this person have insight?" but also, "Are they able to learn from experience? Are they systematically applying their insight?" Knowing the truth will only set you free if you apply it to your life. Jesus taught in parables to protect those who were not at a spiritual level to be able to apply what he taught from the burden of too much knowledge. If we insist on teaching too much too soon to children not ready or able to apply what we teach, we may do them a disservice.

Teaching a person correct principles is a step-by-step process that takes proper communication, patience, and long-suffering. There will often be a fair amount of weeping, wailing, and gnashing of teeth by the student who is trying to learn as well as by the parent who is trying to be patient in the teaching process. Anyone who has been around a friend or relative who has just returned from surgery knows that because of the pain they can be demanding and self-centered. Psychic pain causes the same reaction. We must be prepared to be patient and understanding.

In teaching correct principles it is important to avoid war games. No one really wins a war within a family. I have seen too many wonderful families torn apart because individuals have gone to war with each other. Immediate and extended family are alienated and embittered by accusing and ego-oriented questions such as: "Don't you feel family members should tell each other their whereabouts?" "Don't you think people should act trustworthy so they can be trusted?" "Shouldn't children respect their parents?" "Shouldn't people pay back money they owe?" Such questions are usually loaded. They are asked in a *negative* spirit and no answer is the right answer to bring peace to the relationship or to the individuals involved.

I am not making light of the above values or principles; I just want to point out that principles couched as questions turn what was a solvable problem into a crisis situation because the problem is being approached in a judgmental and rigid style. Family disputes become wars. The focus shifts from understanding and resolution to winning. Guardedness, secretiveness, deviousness, suspiciousness, anger, and one-upmanship prevail. Family wars, like nuclear wars, are unwinnable.

The problem with eliminating the egocentrism that leads to family wars is that egocentrism is itself merely an extreme version of a healthy and necessary *self-governance*. It is critical to remember that the real objective in families and in all human relationships is to have people govern themselves.

The Lord, knowing the difficulties that would arise for those trying to teach correct principles, but letting them govern themselves, reminds us that this is done with " . . . persuasion, by long-suffering, by gentleness, and meekness and by love unfeigned; By kindness and pure knowledge." (D&C 121:41–42.) And then we come to a most important concept in dealing with opposition of any kind, "Reproving betimes with sharpness, *when moved upon by the Holy Ghost*; and then showing forth afterwards an increase of love toward him whom thou hast reproved, *lest he esteem thee to be his enemy*. (D&C 121: 43, emphasis added.)

I am confident that many of us "reprove betimes with sharpness," and I am just as confident that I am not the only one who has done this without the guidance of the Holy Ghost. The kind of sharpness referred to here has nothing to do with harshness, but means "focused." We get a sharp, clear picture when the camera lens is focused correctly. We get a positive result if we focus immediately on the problem at hand and refuse to ignore it or let it fester like an old wound. Then if we follow the Spirit's direction we will know what kind of reproof will help and not hinder. The natural man does not show forth an increase in love after reproving, and the natural man is inclined to reprove in ways that hurt the individual and damage the relationship. Verse thirty-seven makes it quite clear that when we reprove *without* the guidance of the Holy Ghost—in other words, in anger—"the heavens withdraw themselves; the Spirit of the Lord is grieved." Then those who we were trying to teach perceive us as enemies. It is important that parents pray for help and patiently watch for teaching moments instead of using "unrighteous dominion" to set up long-term punishments, which cause resentment and lead only to further opposition and entanglements.

When young people resort to outright war with parents, and parents succumb to the temptation to resort to force, everyone ends up with a no-win situation. I see too many cases of parents playing vigilant watchdog and detective—dealing out more and more restrictive rules while the children become increasingly devious, sneaky, and scheming.

So you may ask, isn't there an effective way to control behavior within the bounds of correct principles? In reference to controlling behavior, there are two types of restraints: external and internal. External restraints cause us to avoid something simply from the fear of getting caught. For example, we don't shoplift because of the floorwalkers, cameras, and one-way mirrors. However, if external restraints are the only restraints, we will eventually be in a situation where we feel we have no one watching and we can get away with something. Internal restraints are the real insulators against wrong doing. These internal restraints are rooted in love, self-esteem, self-discipline, respect, conscience, honor, and the Holy Ghost. Wise parents are adept at helping their children gradually internalize values that act as their restraints and lead to a joyful life.

Dealing with Oppositional People

Oppositional people are difficult to get along with. They often do things that hurt themselves just to spite someone else. They usually generate suspicion, resentment, and anger on the part of those who have to deal with their behavior.

Oppositional people, who often act in the passive–aggressive mode, don't confront and attack openly, but will usually attack in secret. Passive-aggressive spouses find indirect ways of hurting those with whom they are angry. A wife, in her shopping, may forget to get things that she knows may be meaningful or pleasing to her husband. The husband, in turn, may not take out the garbage, or fix the car, as his wife wishes. In this way, he attempts to get even with her.

Before the age of eighteen, people are usually diagnosed only as being oppositional, rather than passive-aggressive. An oppositional youth has ways of attacking from behind to get even with someone, but in doing so he often hurts himself in deep-seated ways. For example, a young person might go out and smoke in the school parking lot, saying to himself, "If my parents could see me now, it would show them." The parents may not actually see it, but in his mind they do, and his behavior is hurting them deeply. In actuality, he is hurting himself. The biggest danger of this pattern is that being oppositional can become a personality style of passive aggression.

Oppositional people often bait others into arguments. If there is a rule, they usually try to violate it. If a suggestion is made, they are against it. If asked to do something, they refuse. If asked to refrain from an act, they feel obliged to carry it out. Ironically these types of people usually do not regard themselves as oppositional; rather, they see the problem as rooted in the unreasonable demands of others. The situation usually causes more distress for the people around them than for the oppositional people themselves.

There are certain ways of protecting yourself from oppositional people, which in turn helps them. When dealing with oppositional people, you really have only two basic alternatives. The first is to "skate." (I will explain this term momentarily.) This method is especially useful when children or youth start coming up with provocative statements specifically designed to denigrate their parents' values. They are not interested in having a learning experience; they just want to be provocative and oppositional—about the Church, about one of the parents, about their homes, their clothes, their father's work, etc.

Some examples of provocative, oppositional statements:

1. "We'd have a better lifestyle if Dad wasn't so stupid."
2. "One of my friends at school told me that Joseph Smith was an epileptic and probably was just mentally ill."
3. "What? And have my friends meet my father? What do you think I am, stupid?"
4. "John gets to stay out as late as he wants to. His parents trust him."
5. "You can make me go to church, but I'll just hate it. Do you feel good about *making* me go to church?"
6. "John's father didn't even graduate from high school, and look how much money he makes."

When young people come up with these types of comments, parents must understand that the children are trying to break away from dependency. It is vital that we refuse to climb into the combative ring with them when they are acting this way. It is effective to maintain as positive a relationship with them as you possibly can—to avoid negative, counterproductive arguments.

When you are being baited for an argument or an intense discussion that you know from past experience will lead nowhere, "skate." Modern politicians seldom really take a stand on anything. Even when they are badgered or provoked by people on some issue, they skate. If you ask a politician what his stand is on the MX missile, you'll get something like, "Certainly we cannot ignore national defense as one of our priorities, but we need to take this into consideration with many other choices and try to make a rational decision. We must make sure that we evaluate all of our priorities and take proper consideration of all things." The politician basically said nothing. When we are confronted with someone whom we know to be oppositional, so should we also say nothing, *at that particular time.*

It is difficult not to take the bait and succumb to the argument the oppositional person dearly wants, but the following ten comments and short sentences seem to adapt themselves to use in skating away from a confrontation:

1. "Whatever."
2. "There seems to be some insight there."
3. "That's interesting."
4. "That is a problem all right."
5. "Ah-ha!"
6. "Reality is often painful."
7. "Oh, really?"
8. "Thank you for sharing."
9. "That's an idea."
10. "It is difficult at times."

Oppositional people have chips on their shoulders. Whatever side of the track you choose to ride, you will find them on the opposite side. At some point, most parents come to believe the scripture should read, "There *will* be opposition in all things." All young people fighting for their independence will become somewhat oppositional from time to time. In fact, as we stated, they *need* to assert themselves and their independence; however, opposition should not become their sole mode of behavior. We can help them avoid the oppositional whirlpool if we do not allow ourselves to react to their baits and traps.

The second alternative in handling oppositional people is more difficult and takes some pre-planning. The psychological term is "paradoxical intention," but you know it by its more common name "reverse psychology."

I once used the technique on one of my sons when he was fifteen and in a constant state of opposition. My wife and I had talked for some time about having him go and pick pineapples in Hawaii. We thought it would be a good educational experience for him and a good break for the whole family. One day my wife called and said my son had a brochure about work in the pineapple fields and that he intended to talk to me about it that night. Realizing the oppositional state of my son, I took advantage of the advance warning and thought through the situation. That night he came in and dropped the brochures in front of me and said, "What do you think of this?" I looked at them for a moment and quietly announced that I had heard of the program and that I had serious reservations concerning it. "Like, what's wrong with it?" he asked. I said that it might break up the continuity of the family. He argued that it would make the family tighter and more closely bonded. I pointed out that the money he earned might just be squandered. He assured me of the farm's disciplinary practices, which literally forced the kids to save their money. I mentioned that many of the kids wanted to leave after only a week or two on the farm. He said that would never happen to him. We continued along these lines for some time until he "argued" himself into the program.

Remember: paradoxical intention only works in those isolated cases where the young person doesn't know what your preferences are and when you have time to think the situation through very carefully.

Overall, it is best to handle oppositional people by skating. The point is to stay out of the combative ring where progress is rarely made. Try to avoid letting your own feelings take over your good judgement. Avoiding an argument with an oppositional person means avoiding his control; *swim past the bait* and wait for a better teaching opportunity because, in a state of opposition, no one learns much.

To learn, people must be willing to accept criticism. However, when people are in a state of opposition, their only inclination is to defend themselves. If we can take the soft approach with children, there opportune times will come when we *can* slip in our principles and make our points.

Good teachers realize that the world outside their classroom is no vacuum. But parents sometimes forget that they are not the only variable in their children's lives. Our children have many contacts, few of which parents can control. We do not have control over a child's teachers, youth leaders, neighborhood friends, or school peers. It is important to realize that because of all these other influences, many children wander away from the gospel for a time. Very often, *if they have been taught correct principles*, they come back.

However, certain children seem to have, from an early age, a *willful intent* not to live the rules and not to follow what they have been taught. I have met many grieving mothers and fathers who came in feeling inadequate and feeling that they, the parents, were totally at fault. Because of the reality of free agency, taking the complete blame for a child's actions is not reasonable and may well lead to depression and feelings of failure.

Many people have lived good, righteous lives and have done very good jobs as parents and still have their children go astray. But even Heavenly Father and Heavenly Mother lost a third of their children. Even their perfect love was not sufficient to hold them all on a true course. They lost the third over a philosophical difference on the question of free-agency, which Satan, that silver-tongued spirit, convinced many was too great a risk.

Influencing Others

When we consider people who as children were emotionally impoverished or had very poor adult role models and yet still seem to do very well in life, we have to ask ourselves, "Why?" One explanation can be the tendencies they brought with them from the preexistence. But invariably in such cases, we can find one or two outstanding significant "others" who positively influenced them. The young person says to himself, "I want to be like this teacher, this bishop, or this advisor."

When we look at our relationships with people who have affected our lives and helped us develop our beliefs about ourselves and life, we see four major variables that have affected their influence on us: frequency, duration, intensity, and desire for change. Frequency of association is imprtant and probably the most emphasized. If a person has frequent contact with another, the likelihood of a major impact or influence increases significantly.

Intensity is the second most important determinant. I think the energy level, bonding, and identification between two people is, in fact, the most important factor in relating to someone else. Most of us can name people whom we have known for years and whom we may even see quite frequently, but with whom the identification and the energy flow just isn't there. Of all the variables, intensity goes farthest in describing the quality of the relationship.

To use the Church for an example, youth leaders are usually selected because it is felt they will be good role models with whom the youth may identify. This has, at times, created problems for some parents when their children constantly extol an advisor. Of course, we as parents would be wise to recognize our feelings of jealousy, recognize the great benefits of positive role models for our children, and recognize, finally, that during some phases of life it is not the "in thing" to identify with a parent.

My parents died when I was quite young, and thereafter I lived with foster parents. One day, when I was fifteen, I came home and found all my belongings packed up. I was told I would be moving to another place. I was not very active in the Church, but even in my desperation, I sensed that Church leaders could be trusted. I went to my bishop, Lyle Peterson, who, after hearing my story, became my legal guardian. Because of his own large family, I could not stay with him, but from that time on I was referred to as one of his sons, and he oversaw and directed my care. He became so important to me that I modeled much of my life after him. He was a very busy man and quite often he was not there. But although the frequency was low, the energy, identification, and modeling were powerful and he has strongly affected my life. I will always be grateful to him and his family for extending themselves to me.

The third variable is duration. Predictably, if we know someone over a long period of time, the likelihood of influencing them is greater. How often have we seen a husband and wife who have been married for a large number of years and who seem to be very much alike?

Finally, the desire for change is the most important variable. I enjoy the following illustration of this:

> Question: How many psychologists does it take to change a light bulb?
>
> Answer: Only one, but the light bulb has to really want to change.

I have already mentioned my belief that we choose some of our own models of identification, but ample opportunity exits for helping someone in the process of change, even if the help is as simple as a clarification of options. For some people, only a crisis can precipitate change. But for others, it is a much quieter process. One of my best experiences in the mission field in Sweden involved the latter.

My companion and I began to teach a man who was severely alcoholic. He was a bachelor who often holed up in his dirty apartment. By teaching him the gospel we showed him some new options in life. He was baptized just before I was transferred to another city. Six months later I returned to the city where this man lived. When I met him again I did not recognize him until he threw his arms around me and embraced me. The familiar physical symptoms of alcoholism had disappeared—he was cheerful and was surrounded by friends. He had chosen an entirely new lifestyle. The change was his own doing. All we had done was present an alternative way of life that he had not been aware of. He had done the rest because his desire for change was great enough.

When Is Helping Helpful?

We are commanded by our Savior to extend ourselves to other people. However, a real question we must address whenever we are helping anyone, whether it is our children or others is, Just how much should we help another?

We often enable people to continue their inappropriate behaviors by doing too much rescuing, helping, and extending. It is possible to jump in and solve other people's problems for them in a way that keeps them weak. I see people rescued to the point that it actually makes them handicapped. Even the Church's welfare program, superb when implemented correctly, is not immune to this problem.

The insight we must remember is that *dependency breeds* hostility. Anytime people become too dependent, whether physically, emotionally, or financially, they eventually become hostile. This hostility is directed to the ones upon whom they are most dependent.

If we look at the countries that America has allowed to become too dependent, we notice that they are the ones that get the most angry with us, often demonstrating against us in the streets. We Americans become very upset and angry with these countries, but we need to realize that we have created a dependency in them that has turned to hostility and has now come back to haunt us. As parents and counselors, we need to realize that if we create in our children or patients too great of a dependency upon us, it will eventually hurt us and the very people we are trying to help.

In attempting to avoid creating dependency, let look at three levels of working with people: intervention, evaluation, and therapy. The three levels are not completely distinct, but each has unique qualities.

The intervention stage, the initial level where the helping process starts, may promote mixed or paradoxical feelings. For example, a woman may appreciate the bishop's help or the meals the Relief Society president brings, but she may likewise feel embarrassed or angry at her inability to reciprocate. This level of service is usually short, and it is oriented toward dealing with an immediate crisis. During this time, the energy that comes from the intervention may likely set the trend for the remaining interactions.

In extreme cases, this level requires the intervening person to have the courage to be very direct. Protective services or legal circumstances may take precedence over good communication and ego protection. While it is important to try to preserve relationships and esteem, life and the protection of people take first place.

Evaluation is the level where we explore all the critical options of different therapeutic directions and resources that the person needing help might turn to. Unfortunately, some people only want temporary intervention measures and try to resist avenues that could facilitate permanent change. These situations are nightmares for bishops and other ward leaders as well as counselors. Evaluation helps us determine whether the person just wants a bandage or whether he really seeks permanent change.

The therapeutic level occurs where and when the person orients himself toward change. Goals are established and actively pursued. Only at this stage do people truly establish a real orientation to feel and act differently.

The therapeutic level is also the stage in the process of helping others where some of the most challenging dilemmas arise. Primary among them is the question of how to help without increasing dependency. Dependency begins from the day of conception. There is nothing wrong with some dependency, but it must be limited. Have you ever seen a chicken hatch from an egg? It's a gruesome process. The chicken has to peck and scratch and push with its wings to get free. When it finally does get out it looks as though it would be better off dead. Our natural inclination may be to crack the egg and assist the bird in its struggle. But if we do, the bird will probably die. The struggle to get free is one of the things that makes the chick tough enough to live. Without this strength, the chick may be too weak, and the other chickens may peck it to death. Similarly, people have to fight against dependencies and have to be allowed to fight some of their own battles and gain strength through their own struggles.

Patients, because of the nature of their relationship with a therapist, often foster dependency. Friends and teachers can certainly do the same. But creating dependency happens when people try to control others and hostility is the inevitable result. Even in cases where the person thrives on the dependency and seems to enjoy it, there is a type of underlying hostility. It may be manifested only in somatic problems like gastrointestinal troubles, ulcers, headaches, or high blood pressure, or it may come out as passive-aggressiveness. Whatever its form, the hostility is there, and it will be evident.

Dependence-based hostility often shows up as a kind of quiet unhappiness directed toward the self or against those depended upon. Sadly, this unhappiness does not necessarily decrease as we try to decrease the dependency. Church leaders see many in the welfare system become angry and upset because their dependence upon the Church has gone on too long. Yet their anger may actually increase as the bishop encourages the person to get out and do something to gain employment.

It will strike some as strange that in a chapter entitled "Helping Others" I have written so much about the dangers of inappropriate helping. I believe that the ability to extend ourselves to others is vital for our very salvation. I have focused on dependency precisely because the ability to give help without creating dependency is just as vital to our salvation. Each of us must learn to extend ourselves in a way that enables others to gain the independence necessary to have joy in life.

In order to avoid creating dependency in the people we help, we must learn how to let go of unrighteous control. It takes sensitivity and understanding to know when and how to help. Perhaps the following guidelines can help us understand when and how to let go of our children as well as others whom we are trying to help:

Letting Go

LETTING GO does not mean to stop caring—it means to stop taking responsibility for someone else.

LETTING GO is not to cut myself off from others—it's realizing I can't control others.

LETTING GO is not to enable others—it's to allow learning from natural consequences.

LETTING GO is not to try to change or blame others—it's to make the most of myself.

LETTING GO is not to care for—it's to care about.

LETTING GO is not to fix—it's to be supportive.

LETTING GO is not to be in the middle arranging—it's to be on the sidelines cheering.

LETTING GO is not to be protective—it's to permit another to face reality.

LETTING GO is not to deny—it's to accept.

LETTING GO is not to nag, scold or argue—it's to search out my own shortcomings and correct them.

LETTING GO is not to adjust everything to my desires—it's to take each day as it comes and cherish myself in it.

LETTING GO is not to criticize and regulate others—it's to be what I can become.

LETTING GO is not to regret the past—it's to grow and live for the future.

LETTING GO is to admit my own powerlessness, which means the outcome is not in my hands.

LETTING GO is to fear less and love more.

For me, the journey I'm on becomes lighter just by remembering it is important to LET GO

Author Unknown

This piece, also has a very important message:

Comes the Dawn

After a while you learn the subtle difference
Between holding hands and chaining a soul.
And you learn love doesn't mean leaning
And company doesn't mean security.
And you begin to learn that kisses aren't contracts
And presents aren't promises.
And you begin to accept your defeats
With your head up and your eyes ahead
Or the grace of an adult
Not the grief of a child.
And you learn to build all your roads
On today because tomorrow's ground
Is too uncertain, for plans and futures
Have a way of falling down in mid-flight.
After a while you learn that even sunshine
Burns if you ask too much.

So you plant your own garden
And decorate your own soul,
Instead of waiting for someone
To bring you flowers.
And you learn that you really can endure
That you really are strong
And you really have worth.
And you learn and you learn . . .
With every goodbye,
You learn.

—Author Unknown

Sanity Strategy #10

Achieve a Gentle Balance

Reinhold Niebuhr wrote,

> God grant me the serenity to accept the things I cannot change, courage to change the things I can and wisdom to know the difference. Living one day at a time, enjoying one moment at a time. Accepting hardship as a pathway to peace. Taking, as Jesus did, this sinful world as it is, not as I would have it. Trusting that You will make all things right if I surrender to Your will. So that I may be reasonably happy in this life and supremely happy with You forever in the next. AMEN.

I have come to believe that the basic foundation of mental health is finding a gentle balance among life's demands. Mental health is achieved by maintaining balance in our lives and in our relationships. Mental health is a process not a status, and most people find maintaining mental health to be a continuing challenge all their lives.

Healthy adults strive to balance work and play and to meet other responsibilities at the same time. A healthy adult is akin to a well-built house where numerous pillars are incorporated as support systems. Should one of the pillars fail, the others should be able to absorb the excess strain. However, many times when one pillar goes, a person will get discouraged and give up on everything. For example, if a young man who loved tennis were to injure his arm so he could not play tennis, he might be tempted to also stop seeing friends, avoid going to tennis matches, and even stop his participation in other activities. A counselor would encourage him to lean more on the other pillars, such as his religion or family activities for a time, and to take up walking or other activities which are still possible with an injured arm.

For me, work, family, friends, religion, and recreation are all vital pillars in life. However, if one of these should go for any reason, I would hope that I would put more weight on the others. For example, if I were to lose my wife, rather than *giving up* my involvement in church or family activities, I should be encouraged to lean more heavily on my church and my family.

One prerequisite for achieving balance in life is a sense of priority. We need to understand the difference between pillars and paneling. There are very few things that we really *need* in life and very few things we really *have* to do. Our *want* list is enormous, but the list of *necessities* is short. It is all a matter of perceptions and attitudes.

A common problem I see is people who become so overwhelmed trying to do right by everybody else that they forget to take time for themselves. I see many resentful, angry people who say, "I don't have any time for myself. I only have time to do things for others." This resentment leads to a quiet hostility. If these people do manage to do something for themselves, they may feel *guilty* and chastise themselves for doing it.

However, *deprivation and guilt* are simply not congruent with the basic goal that God set for us: "Man is that he might have joy." Therefore, maintaining a balance in life that allows us to *feel* the joy could be considered a priority task—but it is an awesome task. It is as difficult to recognize as it is to accomplish.

For example, one man I know is an incredibly devoted husband and father. When his acquaintances learn that he refuses to work past five o'clock because he wants to spend his mealtimes with the family, they are usually quite impressed. But they may not realize that he is often on Church welfare. In a demanding economic world, flexibility is crucial to maintaining a balance.

Like many others, I have found much inspiration in the following thoughts:

If I Had My Life to Live Over Again

> If I had my life to live over, I'd dare to make more mistakes next time. I would relax. I would limber up. I would be sillier than I have been this trip. I know of very few things I would take seriously. I would be crazier. I would be less hygienic. I would climb more mountains, swim more rivers, and watch more sunsets. I would eat more ice cream and less beans. I would have more actual troubles and fewer imaginary ones. . . . If I had it to do over again, I would go places and do things and travel lighter than I

> have. If I had to live my life over, I would start barefooted earlier in the spring and stay that way later in the fall. I would play hooky more. I wouldn't make such good grades except by accident. I would ride more merry-go-rounds. I'd pick more daisies.
>
> —Nadine Stair (written when 85 years old)

The capacity to distinguish between *needs* and *wants* is one primary element of keeping in balance. Once you recognize your real needs, it is a very healthy attitude to devote time, energy, and resources to meeting them. It is equally important to nurture those relationships most important to your well-being, especially your relationship with yourself.

I have in my office a mobile—one of those hanging structures with a central weight that pulls everything up into balance. The weight at the bottom balances the objects (birds, airplanes etc . . .) that twirl above it. I use the mobile to suggest to people that, in their own identities, they have many relationships. They have a relationship with their spouse, one with their children, one with their in-laws, and they also have a relationship with God. But the most important relationship they have is with themselves. This is demonstrated visually by the mobile when the bottom object is likened to our relationship with ourselves, because if the weight at the bottom of the mobile is disturbed all the other objects are also quickly thrown out of balance and they just flop around. Similarly, if our relationship with ourselves is not in balance, all our other relationships may also be "out of balance." Mental health is a balancing act—an act worth learning if we would experience joy in this life.

Conclusion: To Be Real

In your search for happiness, or whatever you seek, do not forget the quest to know yourself. *You are God's most precious and exciting creation, and you have been created that you might have joy*. Improvement and change takes much time and effort, but you *can* learn and choose to think, feel, and act differently. You can steadily achieve greater and greater consistency with your spirit self, which could be equated with becoming "real." The following excerpt from a children's book is a good summary of what I've tried to present in these pages. It means a lot to me. I hope it speaks to you as well:

> "What is REAL?" asked the Rabbit one day, when they were lying side by side near the nursery fender, before Nana came to tidy the room. "Does it mean having things that buzz inside you

and a stick-out handle?"

"Real isn't how you are made," said the Skin Horse. "It's a thing that happens to you. When a child loves you for a long, long time, not just to play with, but REALLY loves you, then you become Real."

"Does it hurt?" asked the Rabbit.

"Sometimes," said the Skin Horse, for he was always truthful. "When you are Real you don't mind being hurt."

"Does it happen all at once, like being wound up," he asked, "or bit by bit?"

"It doesn't happen all at once," said the Skin Horse. "You become. It takes a long time. That's why it doesn't often happen to people who break easily, or who have sharp edges, or who have to be carefully kept. Generally, by the time you are Real, most of your hair has been loved off, and your eyes drop out and you get loose in the joints and very shabby. But these things don't matter at all, because once you are Real you can't be ugly, except to people who don't understand."

"I suppose *you* are Real?" said the Rabbit. And then he wished he had not said it, for he thought the Skin Horse might be sensitive. But the Skin Horse only smiled.

"The Boy's Uncle made me Real," he said, "That was a great many years ago; but once you are Real you can't become unreal again. It lasts for always."

—Margery Williams in *The Classic Tale* of *the Velveteen Rabbit or How Toys Become Real.*

Index of Descriptive Adjectives

active
accepting
adaptable
adventurous
affectionate
aggressive
alert
aloof
ambitious
anxious
apathetic
appreciative
argumentative
arrogant
artistic
assertive
attractive
awkward
bitter
boastful
bossy
calm
capable
careless
caring
cautious
charming
cheerful
civilized
clear-thinking
clever
coarse
cold
complaining
complicated
conceited
confident
confused
conscientious
conservative
considerate
contented
conventional
cool
cooperative
courageous
cowardly
crude
cruel
curious
cynical
daring
deceitful
defensive
demanding
dependable
dependent
despondent
determined
dignified
discreet
disorderly
dissatisfied
distractible
distrustful
dominant
dull
easygoing
effeminate
efficient
egotistical
emotional
energetic
enterprising
enthusiastic
evasive
extending
excitable
fair-minded
fault-finding
fearful
feminine
fickle
flexible
flirtatious
foolish
forceful
foresighted
forgetful
forgiving
formal
frank
free
friendly
frivolous
frugal
fussy
generous
gentle
gloomy
good-looking
good-natured
greedy
handsome
hard-headed
hard-hearted
hasty
headstrong
healthy
helpful
high-strung
honest
hostile
humorous
hurried
idealistic
imaginative
immature
impatient
impulsive
inconsistent
independent
indifferent
individualistic
industrious
infantile
informal
ingenious
inhibited
insightful
intelligent
interests narrow
interests wide
intolerant
inventive
irresponsible
irritable
jolly
judgmental
kind

lazy
leisurely
logical
loud
loving
loyal
mannerly
masculine
mature
meek
methodical
mild
mischievous
modest
moody
naggy
natural
nervous
noisy
obliging
obnoxious
open
opinionated
opportunistic
optimistic
organized
original
outgoing
outspoken
painstaking
patient
peaceable
persevering
persistent
pessimistic
playful
pleasant
pleasure-seeking
poised
polished
practical
praising
precise
prejudiced
preoccupied
progressive
prudish
quarrelsome
questioning
quick
quiet
quitting
rational
rattlebrained
realistic
reasonable
rebellious
reckless
reflective
relaxed
reliable
resentful
reserved
resourceful
responsible
restless
retiring
rigid
rude
sarcastic
self-centered
self-confident
self-controlled
self-denying
self-pitying
self-punishing
self-seeking
selfish
sensitive
sentimental
serious
severe
sexy
shallow
sharp-witted
show-off
shrewd
shy
silent
simple
sincere
slow
sly
smug
snobbish
sociable
soft-hearted
sophisticated
spineless
spiritual
spontaneous
spunky
stable
steady
stern
stingy
strong
stubborn
submissive
suggestible
sulky
superstitious
suspicious
sympathetic
tactful
tactless
talkative
temperamental
tense
thankless
thorough
thoughtful
thrifty
timid
tolerant
touchy
tough
trusting
unaffected
unambitious
unconventional
undependable
understanding
unemotional
uninhibited
unkind
unrealistic
unscrupulous
unselfish
unstable
vindictive
versatile
vocal
warm
wary
weak
whiny
wholesome
wild
wise
withdrawn
witty
worrying
zany